The TORCH MURDERS

The TORCH MURDERS

The Brutal Slaying of Four Teens in Rural Michigan

JAMES THOMAS MANN

Published by The History Press
An imprint of Arcadia Publishing
Charleston, SC
www.historypress.com

Front cover, top, left to right: Thomas Wheatley, Anna Mae Harrison, Harry Lore and Vivian Gold. *Used with permission of Tribune Content Agency*; *bottom*: A police officer inspects the interior of the car belonging to Thomas Wheatley. *From* Actual Detective.
Back cover, inset: The three killers on display for press photographers. *Used with permission of Tribune Content Agency*; *bottom*: Members of the Michigan National Guard and Wayne County sheriff deputies and Washtenaw County sheriff deputies holding back the mob. *Photo provided by John Hilton of* The Ann Arbor Observer. *Used with permission of Tribune Content Agency.*

First published 2025

Manufactured in the United States

ISBN 9781467158756
Hardcover ISBN 9781540299949

Library of Congress Control Number: 2025941136

Notice: The information in this book is true and complete to the best of our knowledge. It is offered without guarantee on the part of the author or The History Press. The author and The History Press disclaim all liability in connection with the use of this book.

CONTENTS

ACKNOWLEDGEMENTS

The most practical advice I can give to an aspiring writer is to find someone who will read over the early drafts of their work and give good clear feedback. No one can proofread their own work. A second person is needed to see the mistakes, misspellings and those parts that need work. I am fortunate to have such a friend in Dr. Kathryn Ziegler, who read over the drafts and with her corrections and suggestions helped improve the final work.

This is a story that requires images to be understood. It is one thing to say a car was burned, but one needs to see a photograph of the vehicle to understand how damaged the car was. There is also the need to show the victims as they were when alive, to make these people not just letters on the page but also human beings. For this reason, I am grateful for the sources that provided the photographs that help to tell the story.

The Detroit Daily Mirror was a daily morning tabloid newspaper owned by the *Chicago Tribune* from 1931 until it was suddenly closed in 1932. The photographs used by the *Tribune* in its reporting of the murders were attributed to the *Mirror*. As the *Mirror* was owned by the *Tribune*, the copyright is the property of the *Tribune*. I have permission to use the photographs from the *Mirror* to illustrate the story of the murders and the events that followed.

Sometimes photographs about the murders attributed to *The Detroit Daily Mirror* appear for sale on eBay. The *Ann Arbor Observer* purchased six photographs off eBay in 2017. John Hilton, editor of the *Ann Arbor Observer*, has permitted me to use these images in this work.

Acknowledgements

George Hagenauer, collector of true crime magazines, was kind enough to scan the story "Trailing the Torch Killers" by Floyd R. Russell from the October 1938 issue of *Actual Detective*. The photographs from the issue are most likely from the case file of the Washtenaw County Sheriff Department.

Tom Quigley, a volunteer at the Ypsilanti Historical Archives, scanned several photographs for use in this work. As always, his work is of the highest quality.

I am also grateful for the support for this project from the Ypsilanti Historical Society Board of Trustees, as this was a great help to me.

INTRODUCTION

When friends gather in the Ann Arbor–Ypsilanti area of Michigan, sometimes the subject of conversation turns to historic murders. During such a conversation, one name that will certainly be mentioned is John Norman Collins, who was convicted of the murder of Karen Sue Beineman in 1970. She was the last victim of the so-called Co-Ed Killer, who terrorized the area during the late 1960s. The memory of these murders hangs like a fading cloud over the community, overshadowing the memory of crimes from years before.

Perhaps the most sensational of these past crimes was the Torch Murders of August 1931, when the remains of four teenagers, charred almost beyond recognition, were found in a still-burning car. At the time, this was called the most gruesome murder in the history of Michigan, perhaps the most gruesome in the history of the United States.

The crime of murder holds a fascination, as the taking of a human life is the ultimate crime. Because of death, all the victim, or victims, could have done or been in their lives will never be. The victims of the Torch Murders were in their mid-teens.

Had they lived, they could, in the normal course of events, have married, had children and grown old. Their early deaths meant they would never meet the people they might have married or had the children they would have raised. The grandchildren they would have seen were never born. This is the true crime of murder, as it ends everything.

Those who know of the Torch Murders will recall the story of how Harry Bennett, the head of the Ford Motor Company Service Department,

Henry Ford's private police force, was told the name of a suspect, captured the suspect, carried him off to his castle overlooking the Huron River and tortured a confession out of him. Bennett would later say this action was justified, as it prevented a miscarriage of justice. This story is most likely a myth, made up by Bennett, to enhance his image as a tough guy. There is much more to the story of the Torch Murders than a myth.

This account of the Torch Murders is based on newspaper reports published as the story unfolded. These reports covered the investigation as it occurred, providing details as the facts were uncovered. The depth of this reporting would be unthinkable today, as concerns over legal issues, premature release of evidence, the rights of defendants and others would influence decisions over what is printed.

This was also the time of the Great Depression and the end of Prohibition as well as a time of open racism. Each of these would play a role in the unfolding story.

The story does not end with the arrest of the killers but continues with the events of what happened after. The murders affected the lives of the families and friends of the dead for years to come. People change over time, sometimes for the better. The troublesome juvenile delinquent can grow into responsible adults. Sometimes, it is in the darkness of life that we find redemption.

1

BODIES FOUND

At about 4:30 a.m. on Tuesday, August 11, 1931, Harvey Santure awoke to see the reflection of flames in a window of his farmhouse. A veteran of the First World War, Santure lived on a farm in the southeast corner of Washtenaw County, Michigan, near the boundary with Wayne County and close to the village of Willis. Thinking a neighboring farmhouse was on fire, he dressed and hurried out. Santure made his way to the site of the flames, about half a mile from his farm. There, on County Line Road, now Rawsonville Road, the boundary between Washtenaw and Wayne Counties, he found a car in flames. Inside the car, Santure saw two bodies in the front seat and perhaps a third in the rear seat. There were, in fact, four bodies in the car. Santure went to the nearby home of his nephew Guy Santure and with him returned to the burning vehicle. The two could not go near the car because of the heat. The windows were closed, but soon the glass began to break from the heat.

Before returning to the car, they had called Harry Aggia, deputy sheriff at Belleville. Dr. Edwin Ganzhorn, who was the coroner for Washtenaw County, was notified as well. A call was made to Washtenaw County Sheriff Jacob Andres, who set out for the site at once with Deputy Sheriff Lynn Squires.

Andres was an experienced law enforcement officer who had served for six years on the Ann Arbor City Police Department, followed by two years as a deputy sheriff and two years as undersheriff. He had been elected to the office of Washtenaw County sheriff the year before.

Top: The car belonging to Thomas Wheatley was parked on the Wayne County side of the road, but the four victims were from the Washtenaw County side of the road. This resulted in the question of which jurisdiction the case fell within. *From* Actual Detective.

Bottom: A police officer inspects the interior of the car belonging to Thomas Wheatley. *From* Actual Detective.

Opposite: A view of the interior of the car in which the bodies were found, showing the extent of damage done by the flames. *Used with permission of Tribune Content Agency*.

Lynn Squires was an experienced detective with the Washtenaw County Sheriff Department who had been employed on several high-profile cases over the years.

When Andres and Squires arrived on the scene, the fire had, for the most part, burned itself out. Flames were still smoldering at the right rear wheel. The interior of the car was completely burned, and the exterior of the car was damaged, as was the roof. The front end of the car was only slightly damaged, and the motor appeared to be in running condition.

Andres and Squires approached the car on the left side and saw a huddled form near the driver's seat with the head leaning toward the left door. Opposite that body was a second body, smaller in stature, lying lengthwise with the head toward the rear of the car. The head of this body was almost on a third body. A fourth body was lying face down where the seat had been.

Inside the car, the bodies were a charred mass, with the leg bones burned to the knees and the arms burned to the elbow. "Only a bare skeleton of the shape of the bodies remained," reported the *Daily Ypsilanti Press* of Wednesday, August 12, 1931.

The bodies, said Dr. Ganzhorn, had most likely been saturated with oil or gasoline and set afire. He based his conclusion on the state of the remains.

Tire marks in the dirt road indicated to police that the car had come from the south, and a long skid track showed the car had come to a sudden stop. Investigators wondered if a second car had passed the car, turned around and forced it to stop. Traces of a struggle were found on the east side of the road, where grass had been trampled down, some brush was broken, and

A pathological examination was needed to determine which were the boys and which were the girls. Note the human bone amid the ashes. *From* Actual Detective.

deep imprints were left in the soil. A small smear of blood was found as well. A woman's shoe with blood on the heel was found nearby; it bore the name Cleveland May Co., a department store in that city.

The bodies were removed after photographs of the scene were taken and transferred to the University of Michigan Hospital for autopsy. A search of the area uncovered more bloodstains on the roadway and on the front bumper of the car. Coroner Ganzhorn collected samples of blood from the scene and sent them to Lansing for examination.

Jules Santure, Harvey's uncle, found a watch that had stopped at 5:06.

One of the first things investigators had to do was determine the identities of the victims.

The car, a Willys, six-cylinder, two-door sedan, was pushed forward, and several articles were found. These included a key holder with two keys on it and a belt buckle bearing the letter H. The car was moved to a garage in Belleville.

The front license plate was bent back toward the radiator. From the license plate number, police learned the car was registered to a Harry Wheatley. He had purchased the car two months before for his son Thomas.

At that same time, two fathers in Ypsilanti were searching for their sons.

Early that morning, Bert Lore, who lived on North River Road, had not heard his son Harry stirring about the house, so he got up to check on him. Harry, who was sixteen years of age, was employed at the Koch Dairy and was scheduled to start work early that morning. The senior Lore looked in the boy's bedroom to see he had not returned home, something he had never done before. Concerned, he called the hospitals and police department but received no information. He dressed and walked into the downtown of Ypsilanti. There he met Harry Wheatley, who was searching for his son Thomas, who was seventeen years of age and a close friend of Harry Lore. Thomas Wheatley had never stayed away from home all night before either.

By the early afternoon, Harry Wheatley had identified the remains. The key holder, with two keys attached, belonged to his son Thomas, and the belt buckle with the engraved H he identified as belonging to Harry Lore, the friend of his son. The other two bodies were of Vivian Gold, who was fifteen years of age and cousin of Harry Lore, and Anna Mae Harrison, seventeen years of age and friend of Vivian. They were identified by parts of clothing still clinging to their bodies.

Harry Wheatley told police his son Thomas had left their home early Monday evening and said he was going to attend a meeting of the DeMolay at the Masonic Temple on North Huron River Street. Harry Lore was

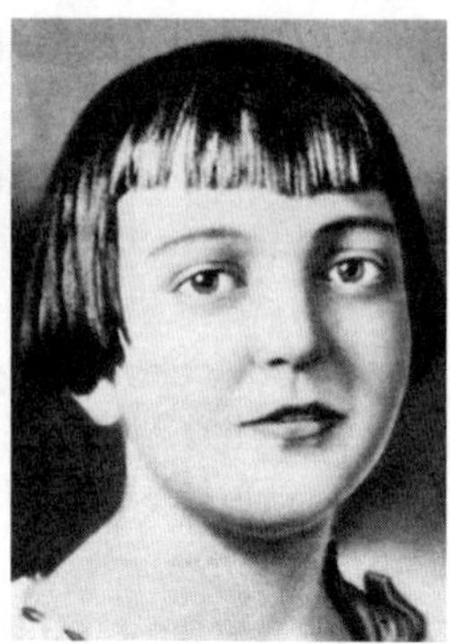

Left to right: Harry Lore, Thomas Wheatley, Vivian Gold and Anna Mae Harrison. *Used with permission of Tribune Content Agency.*

to attend the meeting as well. Lore and Wheatley were both members of DeMolay, a fraternal organization for young men ages twelve to twenty-one who acknowledge a higher spiritual power. When police checked this, it was found no meeting had been scheduled.

Lore and Wheatley were young men of good reputation, known for being honest and hardworking. The two had been friends for years and had been classmates at Ypsilanti High School. The two had left school two years before, in their junior year. Since then, Wheatley had been working with his father on the farm owned by Mrs. W.A. Alban of Belleville, where they had been tenant farmers for fifteen years.

"Thomas was a model boy," said Mrs. Alban. "He left school to help his father and has worked hard ever since."

Vivian Gold and her mother and Vivian's friend Anna Mae Harrison had arrived in Ypsilanti from Cleveland the Saturday before. This was in return for a visit Harry's mother had made to her sister some time before. Harry had asked his longtime friend Thomas Wheatley to help entertain his cousin Vivian and her friend Anna Mae. The boys had taken the girls to Ann Arbor on Saturday to show them the campus of the university. On Sunday night, the boys had taken the girls for a ride around Ypsilanti to visit the interesting and picturesque sites of the city.

The plans for the four for Monday evening are not clear. Lore and Wheatley said they were going to attend a meeting at the DeMolay Lodge Hall. Police later learned the meeting had either been called off or had not been scheduled. Vivian and Anna Mae left the Lore home announcing their intention to see a movie.

At about 8:30 p.m., Wilson Koch, son of Lore's employer, saw the four driving toward the Wuerth Theater on Michigan Avenue. Police assumed the four had gone to the theater to see a movie. The manager of the theater, Glen Harris, said he knew Lore and Wheatley well and they had not entered the theater. The chief usher, Louis Wales, said he was a friend of Lore and Wheatley, and he had stood at his post, just inside the door, all evening and had not seen them.

Vivian Gold and Anna May Harrison said they were going to the Wuerth Theatre on Michigan Avenue in Ypsilanti to see a movie. Instead, they met up with Harry Lore and Thomas Wheatley, who said they were going to a meeting of the DeMolay Society, of which both were members. The two couples ended up in Thomas Wheatley's car in Peninsular Grove, a lover's lane. *Used with permission of the Ypsilanti Historical Society.*

THE KEENE BROTHERS

Police began a search of the area around where the burning car had been found. Some time that afternoon, Corporal Frank Walker of the Michigan State Police and Lynn Squires of the Washtenaw County Sheriff's Department came across a clearing in the woods about half a mile from where the burning car had been found. As the two quietly approached, they saw two men washing clothing in a tub and scraping what appeared to be blood off two heavy wooden clubs. The water in the tub appeared to be bloody.

The two men were the brothers Paul and Lawrence Keene. Paul was forty-nine years of age, and his brother Lawrence was thirty-eight. Their clothing—overalls—noted Walker and Squires, were stained with blood. The two were intoxicated when questioned by Walker and Squires. The Keene brothers lived in a shanty at the clearing, in a two-room "house on wheels" A search of the clearing turned up a barrel of whiskey mash, a bottle of wine, a .22-caliber rifle, a shotgun, a box of .22-caliber shells and two homemade clubs.

The two were taken into custody on suspicion and moved to the Washtenaw County Jail in Ann Arbor. At the jail, Paul Keene, under questioning by Washtenaw County Prosecutor Albert J. Rapp and Assistant Wayne County Prosecutor Milo N. Culchanr, denied knowing anything about the murders. Keene, although dazed by drink, said he could not have seen the flames from his shanty.

As he was being questioned, Paul Keene's shirt was open at the throat, revealing marks on his underwear that might have been made by a bloody hand. At first, he admitted the underwear was his, but when asked about the marks, he denied owning the underwear he was wearing. He said the marks were made not by blood but by shellac. Those who questioned him were doubtful, as there was nothing about the shanty that showed any trace of painting.

Paul Keene said he had lived in the area all his life. He added that he had never been inside a schoolhouse. He and his brother had last been employed about four weeks before, at a nearby sawmill owned by Mark Mason.

His brother Lawrence was taken to the scene of the burned car at 9:00 p.m. by Frank Walker and Washtenaw County Sheriff Jacob B. Andres. There he denied owning a liquor bottle that had been found near the car. At midnight, Lawrence was returned to jail for further questioning.

"These men," Culchanr explained, "are as eccentric to say the least. There is a suspicion of bloodstains on a pair of suspenders, dark gray trousers and a Billy club found in the home. The elder brother says the stains on the clubs are shellac. They both say they were home Monday night and became drunk on a mash used for the manufacture of whiskey. They both tell a disjointed and disconnected story. Paul says he slept alone Monday night and that his brother slept outside under a tree. Paul told us that he had never been in school until he was 26 years old and then only for a visit." Neither of the two brothers knew how to drive a car.

The brothers finally admitted the stains on their clothing and on the clubs were blood—but their own. The two had been in a fight with each other while drunk.

Neighboring farmers told police the brothers were moonshiners and were too lazy and too disinterested to have carried out such a crime.

The clubs and clothing were sent to the Pasteur Institute at the University of Michigan, where Dr. Herbert W. Emerson was to conduct tests on the items.

"Only one thing is certain so far," the *Ann Arbor News* of August 12, 1931, reported Dr. Emerson as saying. "The material on the club which I understand was possessed by the two brothers is blood. Whether it is human blood remains to be shown in tests, which will be conducted this afternoon. The suspected spots on clothing now are being analyzed to determine if they are caused by blood. If they are blood, then they, too, will be subjected to the precipitin tests to determine if the blood is human in origin. The tests to show to which of four classified types of blood on the club belongs cannot be done until late today or even Thursday. This is due to the fact that the condition of blood serum obtained from the bodies is quite unsatisfactory and will require a careful setup of controls to make certain that the results are accurate beyond a doubt."

As the test proved, the blood was human, but the test could not tell whose blood it was.

2

MOTHERS

The dead are not the only victims of murder. An ever-widening circle of family, friends and others are affected by the crime. The pain of loss and guilt over questions that can never be answered are carried by those left behind for the rest of their lives. For some, there will be the unanswerable question, Could I have done something to prevent this? This question, and others, will haunt them until their dying day.

The mother of Vivian Gold was visiting an aunt in Detroit and did not return to the Lore home until late Tuesday afternoon. Arriving at the Lore home, she was puzzled to find the yard filled by reporters, photographers and officers. She made her way to the house, where her sister broke the news to her. She broke down, moaning, "Vivian, Vivian, my baby."

Vivian's mother was carried to a bed, where she lay semiconscious for several hours. "Vivian, Vivian, it can't be!" she cried over and over for several hours. In time she rallied and, sobbing, told of how Vivian had graduated from a junior high school in June and planned to attend John Adams High School in the fall.

"She was such an athletic girl," said Mrs. Gold. "She swam, played all games and wanted to be a gymnasium teacher. We were going to help her. Oh, it is so awful. I don't see how I can stand it. When we said goodbye to Vivian on Saturday, how little we knew we'd never see her again. If I had only made Vivian go with me to Detroit it wouldn't have happened. I am to blame for not making her too. Oh, I can't bear it!"

"My loss is the whole world to me," continued Mrs. Gold as she nervously pulled on a tear-soaked handkerchief. "But I can't forget that Harry is gone, too, and that Anna Mae and the other young man will be here no more. I don't see how I can go on living without Vivian but I'm going to do what I can for Harry's mother."

The mother of Vivian Gold (*center*) after she left the hospital, where she identified the remains of her daughter. She is aided by her sister Maragret Mathies (*left*) and Mrs. Carl Lore (*right*), her sister-in-law. *Used with permission of Tribune Content Agency.*

Mrs. Lore was on the verge of collapse and under a doctor's care. That Tuesday morning, she had identified Harry's body by items of his apparel and had a glimpse of the charred body.

All day, cars were driven past the small house, and a few stopped to give a gift of money or food. "We wanted to help," explained one woman.

The gifts were accepted by Bert Lore, who thanked the donors. Then he returned to his rocking chair to sit beside his wife. "I cannot talk to them," explained Mrs. Lore, her words floating out onto the porch where the donors stood. "I cannot. These questions, these people—I am exhausted."

The mother of Thomas Wheatley sat silently in her chair at the farmhouse near Belleville. She pointed to a clock and said, "See it's eight o'clock. That's the last thing Tom said. He said, 'I'm late. I've milked all the cows, though, mother.' Sometimes he milked all four and sometimes I helped him."

Someone asked if she knew Mrs. Lore.

"Only from hearing Tom tell about her," she replied. "My heart aches for her, though. If I could help her, I would go to her now."

In Cleveland, Hugh Harrison and his wife, the father and stepmother of Anna Mae, were too saddened to travel to Ypsilanti to claim her body. Instead, they waited for the remains to be sent to them. Her father said his life had little meaning for him without his daughter Anna.

Anna, explained her father, had never been away from home before. She was, he said, a happy, quiet, intelligent girl, not one inclined to stay out late. She attended the Third United Brethren of Christ Church near where they lived. It was at the church where she came to know Vivian Gold, and the two had been close friends for years.

Autopsy

Dr. John C. Bugher, instructor of pathology at the University of Michigan medical school, carried out a twelve-hour examination of the bodies at the University hospital.

From the body of Harry Lore, Dr. Burgher removed a .38-caliber bullet from the vertebra. This bullet, Dr. Burger determined, had been fired into the chest. A second bullet had been fired into the right side of the jaw, which tore through blood vessels leading to the heart, causing the free flow of blood. This second bullet had passed through the body and was not recovered. Both bullets had been fired from the same angle.

Lore had also suffered a fractured rib and a punctured lung; a blow from a heavy weapon or kicks with booted feet may have caused these injuries. Police thought it significant that Lore was the only one of the four who had been shot. He was in fine physical shape and big for his age, perhaps the one most likely to put up a fight.

Thomas Wheatley had died as a result of a hemorrhage caused by a fracture in the skull.

Vivian Gold was thought to have died almost instantly from a heavy blow to the skull, crushing it. A quantity of coagulated blood was found within the brain cavity.

A hemorrhage in the ventricles of the brain of Anna Mae Harrison indicated a heavy blow sufficient to cause unconsciousness.

The bodies of the girls were burned beyond recognition, so during the autopsy Dr. Burgher identified them as Body No. 1 and Body No. 2. Their identities were later established only by bits of clothing and jewelry that had survived the flames.

Fragments of a frock printed in a floral design of green, yellow, red and white were removed from the body of Gold, the smaller of the two girls. A lavaliere with a white stone pendant was found still clinging around her neck.

Anna Mae Harrison had been wearing a brown broadcloth dress, fragments of which were found still clinging to the body. She was also wearing a necklace with green and white beads, which had survived the flames.

At the time, it was announced that insufficient evidence remained to determine whether a criminal assault had been made on the girls.

The bullet removed from the body of Harry Lore was sent to the Detroit Police Department, where Lieutenant Earl Stephens, the department ballistics expert, determined the bullet had been fired from an old-fashioned .38-caliber Iver Johnson revolver. The gun, he further noted, was in bad repair.

As part of the investigation, police raided every known dance hall, roadhouse and blind pig within twenty miles of where the bodies were found. Their thought was the boys had taken the girls to such a place as a lark. There, the police thought the boys might have gotten into a fight. After leaving the place, the idea went, someone followed them, forced the car off the road, killed Lore and Wheatley, assaulted the girls and then murdered them. Then they set the bodies and car on fire. In every place visited by police, officers were assured the couples had not been there. Friends of Lore and Wheatley told the police they would not have taken the girls to such a place as those.

"I knew them both so well," said Cecil Wile, a friend of Lore and Wheatley. "There are some fellows you might think had had a drink, but not Harry and Tom. I've gone to high school with them, and I've played baseball with them. I know. You get to really know fellows when you're playing games with them year after year."

A crowd of one thousand people had gathered outside the county jail while the Keene brothers were being questioned. Additional state police officers were called in from Detroit. The crowd, however, was in a good-natured mood and joked with the prisoners in the jail they could see through the windows. As the hours passed, the crowd began to disperse, with the last leaving after two o'clock in the morning.

GRANDMA'S PANTRY

Investigators working to fill the hours between the times the couples left the Lore house and when their bodies were found uncovered a possible lead at about noon on Wednesday, August 12. Two witnesses placed the young people in Milan between the hours of two and three o'clock in the morning. Milan is about eight miles southwest of the place where the bodies were found.

Thomas Goodridge was a deputy sheriff of Washtenaw County and the night watchman at Milan. He was walking down the street when he saw a car approach from the east. He watched as the car was parked at an angle in front of Grandma's Pantry, an all-night restaurant in the basement of the Stimson hotel. Goodridge observed as a young man, whom he identified as Lore, climbed out of the back seat, stepping over a girl in the front seat to do so. Goodridge said he knew Lore by sight and knew his name was Harry. The young man, Goodridge observed, appeared to be drunk, as he lurched, and his shirt was out and his hair mussed. Goodridge planned to impound the car should the driver be in the same condition.

The two girls and the driver were sober, and the four entered the restaurant. Goodridge noted there were perhaps six other cars parked along the street, but Goodridge saw no one else about at the time. He got up off a bench, continued down the street and turned the corner.

In the rear of the restaurant was Norman England, a nineteen-year-old waiter who did not see the party come in but heard them. A partition divided the restaurant into two rooms; the one on the right contained a lunch counter and the one on the left tables. The lights in the room on the left were out, but one of the four turned the lights on in the left section. Police would conclude that at least one of the four had been there before and knew the layout of the space.

When England entered the room to take their order, he found five people there. The fifth person was a man about thirty years of age. England would later say he was particularly impressed by the appearance of this man because of the striking difference in appearance. The man, England said, was carelessly dressed, a sharp contrast to the others.

After taking their orders, England went back into the kitchen. There, one of the young men, whom he identified as Lore, joined him. This young man seemed to have been sick and had soiled his clothing. He asked England for a towel. England told the young man there were no towels available.

The older man kidded the younger man about not being able to hold his liquor. The young couples were very quiet during the meal. When they left, it was the older man who paid the bill of $1.10.

England heard the motor of the car start and saw the headlights through the windows of the restaurant but could not say if all five had entered the car.

Watchman Goodridge had now turned back onto the street and saw the car back out and turn west. At the intersection, the car swung around and went east.

England told police he identified the couples from a photograph he saw in a newspaper. He failed to identify either of the Keene brothers as the fifth man.

Sheriff deputies received a tip that the Bolog brothers might know something about the murder. The brothers owned a blind pig about half a mile from Grandma's Pantry. The blind pig was described as a house with a bar. Police raided the place, and Mickey Baker, the twenty-one-year-old bartender, was taken into custody. In the blind pig, police found two shotguns, one with seven notches in the stock; a holster for a .45-caliber pistol; a .22-caliber pistol; an old rifle; a box of .38-caliber soft-nose shells; and a box of .22-caliber shells.

When questioned by police, Baker said he had been in Detroit on Monday night. At this, his fifteen-year-old cousin broke into the conversation to say Baker had been in Milan that night. Baker admitted this was true.

Norman England told police Baker was not the man he had seen with the two couples at Grandma's Pantry. Police released Baker, as he was unable to supply them with any information concerning the crime.

Andrew Bolog could tell police nothing of the crime. He said his brother Sigmund was in West Virginia.

That morning, August 12, in Cleveland, detectives had found a twenty-eight-year-old man sleeping in a truck that had just arrived from Chicago. When questioned by detectives, the man said he had no address. He told detectives he had boarded the truck in Chicago while en route to Cleveland. In his pocket was a road map of Michigan, with Ypsilanti marked in pencil. The man said he had been "up in Michigan," but his answers became evasive when asked what he was doing there. Detectives took the man to police headquarters for further questioning.

He was roughly dressed, wearing a cap and tan jacket, and was about five feet, eight inches tall and weighed about 140 pounds. Detectives said he appeared to have a below average mentality.

Detectives wondered if he could have been the stranger seen with the two couples in Grandma's Pantry.

England was asked by investigators to describe the clothing the two couples had been attired in while at Grandma's Pantry and to tell them what they had ordered off the menu. The clothing England described did not match the outfits the four had been wearing that evening. The food England said he had served them did not match what was found in the stomachs of the four during the autopsy.

Investigators now wondered if England was mistaken and the two couples and the man who stopped by Grandma's Pantry were travelers who had nothing to do with the case. Or did England make the story up, to get his name in the papers and add a little excitement to his life? The investigators never reached a conclusion to this question.

3
INVESTIGATION

PURSE

Fred D. Jones, a vacuum cleaner salesman from Ann Arbor, was making a call on Tuesday, August 11, when he saw a purse in the center of Tuttle Hill Road. This about three miles southeast of Ypsilanti and about nine miles from where the bodies were found

Jones stopped to pick up the purse, which had been run over by a car. Near the purse, Jones found a powder puff, a compact, a lipstick, an earring, a small handkerchief and a small elephant ornament. There was a dark stain on the purse, which Jones assumed was from a tomato lying nearby.

Jones most likely knew nothing of the murders until he returned to Ann Arbor that evening, when he read newspaper accounts of the crime. Wednesday morning, Jones turned the purse over to Kyle Ordway, Ypsilanti city council member and hardware dealer, for whom Jones had been working. Ordway turned the purse over to Deputy Sheriff Lynn Squires.

Squires showed the purse to the mothers of Harry Lore and Vivian Gold, most likely at the Lore home on North River Street. The two women stood bravely together, as Squires held it out for them to see. Mrs. Gold recognized the purse as belonging to her daughter, Vivian, and fainted at the sight of the blood-stained object. Once Mrs. Gold regained consciousness, she wept wildly. She gripped the purse with her fingers, and it was with difficulty she was induced to let go of it.

She expressed a wish to have the wristwatch given to Vivian by her parents in June, when she graduated from grade school, returned to her as a keepsake.

"Please ask the coroner to be very careful of it," she begged Squires. "It is the one keepsake I want so badly," she said as tears slipped down her cheeks. "Then there is her little ring with the turquoise in it. She had it since she was a baby. The man will keep them for me safely, won't he? Vivian was so fond of both the ring and the watch. She was so thrilled about the watch she only wore it on special occasions. Those will mean a lot to me in the years to come."

At this, Mrs. Gold covered her face with her hands, thinking of the years ahead without her daughter.

Present at the time was Vera Brown, a reporter for the *Detroit Times*, who noted no one had the heart to tell Mrs. Gold the watch and ring had most likely been turned into twisted metal by the heat of the flames.

"You see," continued Mrs. Gold, "Vivian loved pretty things so. I used to make all of her clothes and she had such pretty dresses. The girls were all dressed up in their nicest summer frocks when they went out Monday night. Vivian in her yellow flowered dress and Anna Mae in green linen, which was new. Being my only child, my baby, I was so glad to sew for her, and be sure she looked nice. Her father and I gave her everything she wanted. That watch was the pride of her life. I want it for a keepsake."

Mrs. Lore did not believe her son and the others were at Grandma's Pantry at two o'clock in the morning. "I don't think my boy was in Milan as they say," she said. "He wasn't drinking. I know. This isn't the usual mother's attitude that her son can do no wrong. My boy didn't drink, and neither did Thomas Wheatley. When the truth is discovered, I believe it will be, God must let it be discovered, it will be proved that the children did not have anything to drink. Of that I am certain."

"If only we could look upon their faces and kiss them good-bye for the last time it would be easier," said Mrs. Lore.

This was a wish that could not be granted because of the condition of the bodies.

That afternoon, Mr. and Mrs. Gold left Ypsilanti to return to their home in Cleveland. They had expressed the hope of being of assistance to Grace Harrison, the mother of Anna Mae. At Cleveland, the families would await the return of their daughters.

"In the meantime," noted the *Detroit Times*, "this university town, usually engrossed at this season with summer school and its students, thinks of nothing else but the gruesome murder which has shocked the state. Hundreds stand day and night about the sheriff's office, on the sidewalk, and in the street. Automobiles cruise by, hoping they may get a glimpse of the criminals if an arrest is made."

This crowd was made up of a cross section of the local population, including professors from the university, local merchants, farmers and housewives, watching the jail for any new developments in the case. Fathers and mothers thought about how it might have been their children who could have been the victims. The young talked about the recent series of automobile holdups that had occurred. The crowd watched as men with shotguns entered and left the building. Everyone talked about the murder; it was an all-consuming topic of conversation. Everyone talked about "swift justice."

The place where the purse was found was known to be frequented by couples holding "petting parties." Deputy Squires expressed the opinion that Wheatley had parked his car at the site and was then surprised by their assailants. The purse, investigators believed, might have fallen or been tossed out of the car during the scuffle. A search of the road and ditch where the purse was found, however, failed to show any evidence of a struggle.

At noon that day, Hazel Pierce, the wife of a former Ypsilanti City police officer, was driving alone on Tuttle Hill to see the site where the purse had been found. As she passed near the site, she was accosted by four rough-looking men who attempted to force her off the road. The men were in a black car with an Ohio license plate. She was unable to read the number off the plate. One of the men got out of their car and tried to leap onto the running board of her car to take hold of the door. She sped past the men, turning onto the roadside and swinging close to the ditch.

On returning to the city, Pierce reported the incident to the police, who set out at once to the site. Officers at the site found no trace of the car described by Pierce.

Toy in Charge

The burned-out car with the charred bodies inside was found on the east side of County Line Road, now Rawsonville Road, marking the boundary between Wayne County and Washtenaw County. The car and bodies were in Wayne County by a matter of a few feet. The victims were from Washtenaw

County. This led to a question of jurisdiction, which law enforcement agency, either in Wayne or Washtenaw County, had responsibility for conducting the investigation. Agencies on both sides of the line began to carry out their own investigations, each pledging cooperation with the others. As the agencies carried on their investigations, there was no organizational structure in place for the needed coordination.

As the investigation progressed, friction developed between the officers of Wayne and Washtenaw Counties. For this reason, Michigan Governor Wilbur M. Brucker ordered State Attorney General Paul W. Voorhies to take complete charge of the investigation.

"There must be complete co-ordination between all law enforcement agencies in Michigan, to effect a speedy solution to this most bestial crime and sure prosecution of the murders," said Governor Brucker in a statement. "It is essential that there should be some one official in authority, to direct the investigation and all criminal procedure. This murder must not go unsolved."

When Voorhies arrived at Ann Arbor on Wednesday afternoon, he found one deputy from Wayne County who did not know what angle to pursue or what angles the others might be working. Confusion, Voorhies said, was evident.

That afternoon, Voorhies held a conference with Washtenaw County Prosecutor Albert Rapp, Wayne County Prosecutor Harry S. Toy, Washtenaw County Sheriff Jacob B. Andres, Sheriff Henry Behrendt of Wayne County, Captain L.A. Lyon of the Michigan State Police and Harry Bennett, head of the Ford Motor Company Service Department, a private police force owned by Henry Ford.

The presence of Harry Bennett at the conference would not have surprised most people living in the Detroit area in 1931. What is not clear is whether Bennett was invited to attend or invited himself. In either case, Bennett would have been seen as a resource for local law enforcement, as he headed the one-thousand-man Service Department of the Ford Motor Company. This was, in effect, a private police force owned by auto magnate Henry Ford and managed by Bennett. The staff of the department included college athletes, former police officers (usually dismissed from the force) and ex-convicts, including some who had been convicted of murder, such as the boxer Kid McCoy.

Bennett was born in 1892 in Ann Arbor. His father died in a barroom brawl while Harry was still an infant. His mother had him sing tenor in the choir of St. Andrew's Episcopal Church. He left home at the age of seventeen to join the navy. In the navy, Bennett became a deep-sea diver and a boxer in the lightweight class, calling himself "Sailor Reese."

In 1917, Bennett began working for the Ford Motor Company at the Rouge River Plant. There he gained the notice of Henry Ford, and by 1919, Bennett was head of the Service Department. The Service Department was responsible for stopping the theft of tools and parts, security, maintaining order and preventing union organization. The men employed under Bennett were tough, their methods often brutal. During the 1920s, Bennett told Henry Ford he would protect the Ford grandchildren from kidnappers.

A small man, five foot, six inches, Bennett was tough and brave. Once, he drove after an escaping thief who had just robbed a Ford office. As Bennett drove, a member of the Service Department rode on the running board of the car, firing a shotgun at the speeding car. Well, at least, that is the story Bennett told.

Bennett was involved in the recovery of ransom money paid to an intermediary in the Jackie Thompson kidnapping case of 1929. The five-year-old Jackie was carried off in front of his home in Detroit. Some $20,000 was entrusted to an intermediary who was to pay the ransom and secure the release of the child. The intermediary, instead, kept the money for himself. Bennett claimed he used underworld connections to locate the intermediary and recover the ransom money. Another man who was involved in the case, identifying the main suspect, was Lynn Squires of the Washtenaw County Sheriff's Department. Jackie was returned to his family, alive and in good health.

By 1930, Bennett lived in a grand house known as the "Castle" located on Geddes Road, between Ann Arbor and Ypsilanti. There he kept adult lions and tigers in the basement.

When the conference was over, it was noted, Bennett and some of his detectives went in pursuit of their own suspects.

At the conference, Sheriff Behrendt said, "My office didn't need the assistance of Washtenaw County officials."

"I was very disappointed when Behrendt spoke as he did," said Voorhies later.

Voorhies set up an office in the Ann Arbor Savings Bank Building, explaining, "Some central head was needed to direct the activities of all persons connected with the investigation, and for this reason I believe a headquarters in Ann Arbor will prove valuable as a clearing house for all information."

At the conference, Voorhies appointed Wayne County Prosecutor Toy as head of the investigation. He noted the case was "more tangled up with Washtenaw" than Wayne, but as the bodies were found in Wayne County, he felt inclined to give jurisdiction to that county.

"I have absolutely no criticism to make of any official in Washtenaw County up to the present time. The only purpose of establishing the headquarters is to secure in some way the apprehension of the persons who committed this dastardly crime. When it is determined where the crime of murder was committed, prosecution will be in whichever county it was committed," stated Voorhies.

Washtenaw County Prosecutor Rapp said the attitude of Prosecutor Toy had been extremely fair.

At the office, equipment such as telephones and stenographers were brought into service at once, to help coordinate the work of investigators from each county, and fifteen troopers from the Michigan State Police.

"Each officer that has taken part in the search is to be brought to headquarters today to make a full statement of his work," explained Deputy Wayne County Prosecutor Culehan.

"The work will be done on the system of a metropolitan police department," continued Culehan. "Every facility will be united into one effort to bring the slayers to justice."

An inquest into the murders was opened at the Washtenaw County Courthouse on Wednesday at 2:00 p.m. under the joint jurisdiction of Wayne County Coroner Albert R. French and Edward C. Ganzhorn, coroner of Washtenaw County. A jury of six farmers was sworn in but did not hear evidence. At the request of Albert Rapp, Washtenaw County prosecutor, the inquest was postponed for one week. The families did not attend the inquest.

Immediately after the close of the inquest, Washtenaw County Sheriff Andres announced the county would receive additional help to be provided by the American Legion. Some months before, a program was started under the auspices of the Legion to add 127 deputy sheriffs to the Washtenaw County force. The plan was for these men to help patrol the highways of the county. These men, all honorably discharged veterans of the First World War, were to be armed with army rifles and one hundred rounds of ammunition. Each man was to be a trained marksman. The program was rushed to completion after the discovery of the bodies. They would soon prove useful.

Officials were following what they hoped to be a promising clue: a white gold wristwatch, missing from the arm of Anna Mae Harrison. Police sent a description of the watch to jewelers throughout the area in the belief the killer would try to pawn or sell the watch.

At about 2:00 p.m. on Wednesday, August 12, an African American woman approached the police desk in the Ypsilanti City Hall, where the police department was located, and handed an officer a slip of paper. On the paper, she had laboriously spelled out the names of those she said were the killers. The slip of paper was, in due course turned, over to Wayne County Prosecutor Harry S. Toy, who was now in charge of the investigation. This prompted Toy and his staff of investigators to make a sudden return to Detroit.

"Mr. Toy closeted with his aides at 2 a.m.," reported the *Detroit Free Press* of Thursday, August 13, "refused to say whether arrests were imminent."

"I can say nothing now," said Toy. "I might spoil everything."

There were no further reports on the names on the slip of paper turned in by the woman.

Shortly before midnight on Wednesday, Maxwell Holly of Ypsilanti told police he had seen Wheatley's car on Huron Street in Ypsilanti between 11:00 and 11:30 p.m. He said he saw Wheatley and the others in the car.

"I waved to them," said Holly, "and they waved back. The car was headed toward the business district."

Somehow a man named Howard Forwalder, who was about twenty-five years of age, came under suspicion as the fifth man at Grandma's Pantry. On the afternoon of Thursday, August 13, his room at the Hawkins House Hotel on Michigan Avenue in Ypsilanti, where he was a boarder, was searched by Lynn Squires of the Washtenaw County Sheriff's Department and Bruce McGlone of the Michigan State Police Post at Wayne. They removed from his room a suitcase of empty wine bottles and two bottles of moonshine. The suitcase was taken to the Ypsilanti City Hall by Harry Bennett of the Ford Motor Company Service Department.

"According to Mrs. Schaff, wife of the proprietor of the hotel," noted the *Ypsilanti Daily Press* of Thursday, August 13, "Forwalder is a steady, hardworking young man. He has worked at the new Ypsilanti State Hospital (then under construction), but of late has been out of employment. She was confident that he had no part in the slaying."

At about 9:30 a.m. on Wednesday, August 12, a man had calmly walked into the pawnshop of Max Frank at 133 Michigan Avenue in Detroit. There the man was paid six dollars for a wristwatch and signed his name as D.F. Blackstone. On the morning of Thursday, August 13, the manager of the shop received the number of the wristwatch missing from the body of Anna Mae Harrison. Comparing the number issued by police to the number on the watch, the manager found the numbers matched. He at once called the police. By this time, Blackstone was undergoing questioning by police at Ypsilanti.

4

GUN

"If I'd done what I wanted to do Monday night," said George Nelms later, "I'd have stuck my knife in Dave Blackstone and those four youngsters would be alive today."

George Nelms was a thirty-one-year-old African American man living at 550 Watling Boulevard on the south side of Ypsilanti, where most of the African American population of the city lived. This was the so-called "Colored" section of the city. Although segregation was not the law in northern cities like Ypsilanti, it was the common practice. The house he lived in was owned by Otis Odem, also African American, who rented a room to Nelms, which he shared with David Blackstone. Blackstone, who was twenty-six years of age, had served two prison sentences for receiving stolen property, one in Missouri and the other in Illinois. Odem also ran a blind pig out of his house as well. Although Nelms and Blackstone shared a room, they were not friends.

Early on the evening of Monday, August 10, 1931, Nelms returned to the room he shared with Blackstone to discover some of his liquor was missing. He accused Blackstone of stealing it, and the two came close to getting into a fight. Odem stepped in to break up the two. "We've had trouble enough up here already: don't you go to fighting and bring us anymore," said Odem.

"We knew before that he was a thief," explained Nelms later. "He had an old model T Ford, without any license plates, that he drove around nights. We asked if it was stolen and he said, 'sure I took it,' so we made him drive it off the premises."

According to Nelms, after he and Blackstone quarreled, Blackstone left the house but returned at about 8:00 p.m. When he returned, Frank Oliver and Fred Smith, both young white men, were at the house. Blackstone was a friend of Smith and Oliver, so the three sat around drinking for a time.

Then Smith left the house. Soon after Mrs. Odem heard someone in the yard behind the house. When Odem and Nelms went out to see who was there, they found Smith trying to steal a car belonging to a white man who had stopped in but had left with someone. Odem and Nelms stopped Smith from stealing the car. Soon after, Smith left the house with Blackstone and Oliver.

"The next time I saw Blackstone was about 11:30," said Nelms. "He came in sort of in a hurry, like, grabbed his gun out from under the mattress and went out, and I didn't see no more until he came in about 5 o'clock. I wouldn't sleep with him no more, so I got up and he went to bed."

"When he left the house, he had a blue shirt on," continued Nelms. "In the morning, he didn't have no shirt, —just his B.V.D.'s and he was so nervous he couldn't button or unbutton them. He had one fresh cut on his finger, but that was all I noticed."

Another who was familiar with Dave Blackstone was Frank Johnson, also African American, who had been at the Odem house the previous Sunday night, August 9, 1931. That night, Blackstone, whom they called "Hot Tamale," because he sold hot tamales on the street, was at the house with Fred Smith. Johnson saw Smith and Blackstone out behind the house, trying to steal a car. "I saw them try to pry open the door with a screwdriver," said Johnson later. "First, they tried one side of the car and then the other. They didn't seem to get no place.

"Then they came into the house, I took 'Hot Tamale' to one side, and I said to him, 'Hot Tamale you don't want to run round with that Smith man and his friend Oliver. They won't do you no good, no how, you wait and see.'

"'Hot Tamale,' he just laughed and told me he could take plenty care of himself. So, I didn't say no more about it to him."

"Well Tuesday everybody is talking about those murders. All day long that's all I heard and read about. And that night when I went to bed, I had a vision. It was a fearful vision, just as clear as a picture. In my vision I saw three men doing those murders out on that lonely road.

"I didn't sleep no more that night, I just couldn't sleep after that vision. And Wednesday morning I got into my clothes early and went right over to Otis Odem's house. Hot Tamale lives at Odem's when he doesn't live with his folks."

Johnson pounded on the door to the house, and when Odem opened it, Johnson asked, "Otis, what time did Hot Tamale get home Tuesday morning?"

Odem told Johnson Blackstone arrived home at about half past five.

"Was he nervous?" asked Johnson.

Odem replied, "He was nervous like anything, all over. When he came home, he didn't walk right in like he always does. Instead, he knocks on the door and ask me can he come in. That strikes me as queer for Hot Tamale to ask, and I tell him course he can come in."

Odem told Johnson Blackstone did not have his shirt on when he arrived home, only his undershirt, and his hat was missing.

Odem and Blackstone had an argument, during which Blackstone dropped a gun onto the floor. Blackstone told Odem, "You can have this, I'm through."

Then Blackstone packed his belongings and left the house.

"He left his rod here?" asked Johnson.

"Wouldn't take it with him," Odem.

"Well," said Johnson, "you better unload that rod."

"What for?" asked Odem.

"Never mind what for," said Johnson. "If you are wise, you will unload that rod."

Later that day, Johnson saw Blackstone on the street and noticed a cut on his right hand. "How come you cut your hand, Hot Tamale?"

Blackstone told Johnson it was an accident.

Then Johnson asked Blackstone, "You hear about those dreadful murders out on that lonesome road, Hot Tamale?"

Blackstone responded with a grunt and then began to shake from head to foot. Then he walked away.

"When Hot Tamale shakes like that, that's when I get my suspicion. 'Here is something I ought to tell Mr. Southard,' I said to myself. So, I starts for the jail. But there's a big crowd in front of the jail. I don't like the looks of that crowd, so I go home.

"But I can't forget that vision. And that suspicion keeps weighing on my mind. So, Wednesday night I decided I go down come anything and see Mr. Southard. And I does."

Mr. Southard was Ralph Southard, the chief of the Ypsilanti City Police Department. His office was on the second floor of the Ypsilanti City Hall on North Huron Street.

Back at the house of Otis Odem, George Nelms had returned home, and Odem showed him the gun. "I don't want this gun," said Odem to Nelms. "You can throw it away or do anything you want with it."

The city of Ypsilanti Police Department of 1931. The Chief of Police Ralph Southard is seated in the front row, second from right. *Used with permission of the Ypsilanti Historical Society.*

"I looked at the gun," said Nelms later, "and sure enough, it had been fired within a day or two. I took a little rag and wiped it and there was fresh smut on it. I got to thinking, and it all came to me, and I told Otis what I thought, and what I was going to do."

As George Johnson was telling his story to Chief Southard, at about 10:30 p.m. on Wednesday, George Nelms entered the office and placed the gun on Southard's desk. The gun was a .38-caliber Iver Johnson, the type of weapon used in the murders. Southard called the Detroit Police Department to request an immediate examination and test of the weapon. Then he sent the gun to Detroit with two men.

The gun was delivered to Lieutenant Earl O. Stephens, the ballistics expert for the Detroit Police Department, by Dan Martin of the Wayne County Prosecutor's Office, at about midnight. Stephens told Martin he needed the fatal bullet that had been removed from the body of Harry Lore to complete the examination. The bullet, Stephens noted, was in the vault of the Wayne County Sheriff's Office property room. Because of the concern the premature revelation of the gun being in police procession could cause the killers to flee, information about the gun was restricted to only a few. This information was even withheld from Wayne County Sheriff Henry Behrendt and his chief deputy, Archie Fraser.

At about the same time the gun was turned over to Stephens in Detroit, Fred Raymond and Harold Truax of Prosecutor's Toy's investigation staff called on Fraser at his hotel room in Ann Arbor. Raymond and Truax asked Fraser to have the bullet turned over to the prosecutor's office.

"They did not indicate there was any particular haste and claimed they did not know in what connection it was wanted," said Fraser later. "Seemingly they were perfectly satisfied when I told them I would see to it that the bullet was turned over to Prosecutor Toy as soon as the office was opened in the morning, 8 or 8:30 o'clock. Soon afterward, they returned and said their chief desired possession of the bullet immediately.

"I called the Detroit office at once and made the arrangements. Even the second time, Raymond and Truax said they did not know the reason for the haste. It was morning before I learned of the finding of the gun. I had to find this out by reading the newspapers."

Prosecutor Toy later claimed the delay in informing the sheriff's office was due to his office being unable to find anyone who could have the safe opened. Wayne County Sheriff Behrendt later stated he was at home in his residence at the jail. He would not know about the finding of the gun until morning.

To carry out the examination, Stephens fired a bullet from the suspect gun into a box filled with wads of cotton. Once the bullet was removed from the box, he placed it on a comparison microscope with the fatal bullet. A comparison microscope is two microscopes with a bridge so two objects, such as two bullets, could be examined at the same time. Stephens peered through the microscope and compared the marks made on each bullet made when passing through the barrel of the gun. The marks were the same, proving this was the murder weapon. Once the exemption was completed, the gun was turned over to Investigator Martin, who then returned to Ypsilanti with the gun.

Lieutenant Stephens called Chief Southard at Ypsilanti at 3:20 a.m. and informed him that this was the weapon used in the murder.

"I went at once to Blackstone's house," said Chief Southard. "I got him out of bed and put him under arrest. I brought him into my office about 5 o'clock Thursday morning. I talked to him for two hours. I couldn't get much out of him. But he told me about a man he had been out with the night of the murder. He said he knew the man as 'Curly' and 'Smitty.'"

"With that as our lead," continued Southard, "it was not hard to find out that the man he meant was Fred Smith. Officers were sent to the Smith farm near Ypsilanti, and before 8 o'clock he was under arrest." The arrest of Fred Smith, it was reported, took place as he was preparing to help with the threshing.

Fred Smith had a criminal record that began in 1927 when he was sixteen years of age. He had been arrested for breaking into a gasoline station. He was placed on probation for five years because his mother was blind. Then in September 1928, he was arrested for violation of probation after stealing an automobile. The minimum term was five years, of which he served two and a half. He was paroled on May 13, 1930, because of good behavior and the needs of his blind mother. He returned to Ypsilanti on May 28, 1930.

He was arrested twice after that during an investigation into the breaking and entering of the Cady gas station. Smith was again arrested on March 8, 1931, after an accident in the family car, which resulted in a fight. At this time, his parents requested he be taken into custody and an examination be held to determine his sanity.

As part of the request the family filed with probate court, his father stated: "He has spells when he does not know what he is doing. He jumps from one thing to another and is very nervous. He sleeps for 15 hours at a time."

Smith, when annoyed, would say, "I'll carve their hearts out." His language was described as abusive and his cursing as vile.

The examination concluded he was sane.

Blackstone and Smith were questioned by police in separate rooms; each admitted they were in Milan at 2:30 a.m. of the morning of the murder. The two said they went to a gambling place with the intention of holding it up. Blackstone said the place was open but the two chose not to attempt a holdup. Smith told police he was disappointed to find the place closed. Smith and Blackstone told police they returned to Ypsilanti by driving on the lonely back roads but were unable to describe the route they traveled. When Blackstone was asked how he came into procession of the murder weapon, he said he "just had it, that's all."

The Ypsilanti Police Department was headquartered in the Ypsilanti City Hall at 300 North Huron Street. This was a large three-story house, built in the Second Empire style, complete with a mansard roof, a projecting tower and tall, narrow windows. The jail was in the basement, and women and juveniles were housed on the upper floors. The justice court was on the second floor. The office of Chief Southard was across the hall from the justice courtroom.

Early Thursday morning a reporter for the *Ypsilanti Daily Press* arrived at city hall, where the reporter saw little activity. Officers had little to say about the case and denied practically everything. Soon, however, word of the arrests leaked out, and the Ypsilanti City Hall became the center of activity. In a short time, nearly one hundred reporters and photographers

Ypsilanti City Hall was in the Second Empire–style house at 300 North Huron Street from 1910 through 1970. The office of Ypsilanti Chief of Police Ralph Southard was at the front of the second floor to the left. *Used with permission of the Ypsilanti Historical Society.*

were assembled around city hall. This was in addition to the growing crowd of locals, which came to number about one thousand, and they were in an increasingly hostile mood.

No official statement was issued until 11:00 a.m., when Miles L Culehan, assistant Wayne County prosecutor, informed reporters of the gun having been tested. Culehan did not explain how the police came into possession of the gun.

At noon, an enterprising young man sold sandwiches to the reporters milling about city hall. Another young man who was in the crowd was then ten-year-old Ed Deake, who later said being present in the crowd that day sparked an interest in law. Later in life, Ed Deake became a lawyer and a judge.

Sometime during the day, Catherine Keller, known as Kate, the twenty-five-year-old "sweetheart" of Fred Smith, turned a shirt over to police. She said it was the shirt Smith was wearing on Monday. Under questioning, Smith and Blackstone told police Kate Keller had been with them for a time on Monday evening. For this reason, the police wanted to question her.

Reporters outside city hall tried to listen in on the questioning of Blackstone, who was undergoing interrogation in the office of Iva Manning, the court stenographer. To frighten Blackstone, officers dropped light bulbs next to his chair. Blackstone was heard to cry, "Ah ain't no murderah, ah never killed nobody. You all is trying to make me a murderah."

The questioning of Blackstone was turned over to Dan Martin and Fred Raymond, special investigators of Wayne County. After hours of questioning, Martin said to Blackstone, "You are a cooker of hot tamales. You burned those girls."

The investigators may have shown Blackstone a crime scene photograph of the charred bodies, perhaps still burning, in the car.

After thirteen hours of questioning, Blackstone broke down and began to cry. Once the investigators finished, Blackstone sat in his chair and wept. Then he made his confession:

"On Monday night we thought we would go and rob a gambling game over at Milan. We got together and went over there, and it didn't look good to us.

"So, we said we would go down Lovers' Lane and knock off some of these here petters. They always is easy. We went down and saw this car, in which Miss Vivian Gold, Miss Anna Mae Harrison, young Wheatley, and Harry Lore were riding.

"We robbed them of some little things and a little bit of money. Then we saw that Lore had recognized us. So, we talked to him about it. The boys said they wouldn't make no complaint and we was for letting them go.

"But Smith he weren't satisfied. He said what about the girls? And then we got ahold of one of the girls and dragged her out of the car. She came out clawing at him.

"We then lined them all up alongside the road and started to frisk them and make them promise not to tell—that was at Tuttle Hill. First thing I knew Smith jerked a pistol out of his pocket and shot three or four times.

"Then we had to shoot them all. We knocked them down and put them in the back of their car and Oliver drove back to Ypsilanti with us. We took our car and got some gasoline while Oliver waited a little way off with the Wheatley car and the bodies.

"After we had our gasoline, we drove back down along the road toward where we left the bodies. On the way we heard one of the girls groan so we hit her in the head with a wrench.

"We was scared they was not dead, so we took rocks and beat them in the heads until, we were sure. Then after we was sure we drove the car off the road and set fire to it. We went right by the Lore home after we had killed those folks with all the bodies in the car."

The confession came between 4:00 and 4:45 p.m.

The questioning of Smith was now being carried out by Prosecutors Rapp and Toy, who told him, "We know you committed the crime. By refusing the details you are only hurting yourself and obstructing justice."

Now Special Investigators Martin and Raymond rushed into the room where Smith was being questioned and shouted at Smith: "We know you did the killing. Blackstone has told us all."

Then Smith said, "If you promise to protect me. I'll take you out and show you just how the crime was committed."

Smith had reason to be concerned about his safety. He could hear the voices from the crowd outside the building and their increasingly violent tone. Words such as *kill* and *lynch* more than likely held his attention. There may have been as many as five thousand lynchings in the United States from the end of Reconstruction in 1877 and well into the 1950s. The majority of those lynched were African Americans, with a smaller number of whites murdered by mobs as well. Lynchings were not confined to the former states of the Confederacy but occurred in northern states, including Michigan, as well.

After Smith had finished his confession, reported the *Detroit Free Press*, he tried to escape by grabbing an iron bar from a table in the room where he was being questioned and attempting to beat his way out. Two deputies, the account reported, quickly overpowered him. The account did not explain why an iron bar was in the room where a man suspected of murder was being questioned.

In 1931, police were under no obligation to inform suspects of their right to remain silent or have an attorney present during questioning. These rights, known as Miranda Warnings, were thirty-six years in the future. Until then, police could use interrogation methods known as the third degree, which could include beating a confession out of a suspect. There are no firsthand accounts of such methods used on Blackstone or Smith, but stories of such were told in the years after.

According to one such story, Blackstone was stripped of his clothing, pushed up against a table and his penis stretched out on the tabletop. Then an officer, it was said, struck the penis repeatedly with a billy club.

There was an office in city hall that had a circular indentation in the wall. The story told among city workers about the cause of the indentation was Blackstone's head being repeatedly knocked against the wall.

Reporters located Kate Keller, the "sweetheart" of Smith, at 407 Campbell Avenue that evening, where she had been staying. There she made a statement to reporters. She said:

> *I took the clothes Fred Smith was wearing Monday night up to the officers to show that there was no blood on them. I don't believe the boy did this thing but that he was bluffed and scared in "confessing." I have been sorry for him because everyone seemed to have it in for him. Ever since he was led into trouble by other boys who slipped out of punishment, and served a term, the authorities have had it in for him. I saw him for a minute Monday about 6:30 in the evening, when he went past here and stopped a moment. He did not ask me to go out with him that night. But I saw what suit he wore, as I said, so I went to his room and got the clothing. His mother, who is blind, is also convinced that Fred did not do this thing. I have seen him since Monday night, and he did not seem disturbed or any different from usual. I am sure that he was not guilty.*

In the end, both Blackstone and Smith confessed to the murders, and Smith did show the investigators how the murders were committed.

Sheriff Andres later said, "Smith took us out and explained many of the details, although his confession was what you would call garbled."

The *Ann Arbor Tribune* published the full confession on Friday, August 14, 1931:

> *We started Monday night about 9 o'clock and took Kate home, goes and gets Blackstone. Kid leaves Odis Oden. Drove to Frank Oliver, 1250 Hawthorne subdivision. Goes out Ecorse Road and we got his car and went looking for a stick-up. The nigger had the gun. Blackstone and us started out with the old Tudor car. Went all around the county. The boys were parked in paper mill grove, had a blanket on the ground. Blackstone puts gun on Wheatley and Smith drives Wheatley's car. Drove to the end of the road. Blackstone took them down in Tuttle Hill. Blackstone assaulted the largest girl, hit her with his fist, shot at Smith, walks back and shot both of the boys, four shots. Blackstone picked a small can and drained it out of the tank, poured two cans of gas over them and Frank Oliver got under biggest girl, and she was breathing. He dragged her out of the car and kicked her in the face. Then throwed her back in the car. Set fire to the car by lighting a handkerchief. At 10 minutes to five the fire was started. Then we went to county line, then went home. This is my confession.*

Frederick D. Smith signed the confession. The witnesses to the confession were: James I. Wanzeck, Fred Freedman, Harry Bennett and H.D. Truan.

"I can't believe Fred Smith would kill my boy," said Bert Lore when told Smith had confessed to the murder of his son Harry. "They went fishing together when they were kids."

"Fred was a fairly good boy until he got mixed up with a bunch that were stripping automobiles," continued Lore. "He wasn't a bad little fellow. He played with my boy. We noted a change in Smith after he came back from Ionia. He was hard-boiled and got angry at the least little thing. Still, I can't believe he killed my boy."

"Both of the kids were crazy about fishing," Lore recalled. "They used to pick up a family friend of ours, Edward Burk, and the three would go over to the Irish Hills. Then the Smiths lived near us, just a few houses away from here on Huron Road. Two years ago, they moved away, when the father George Smith, brought a farm on Textile Road five miles outside Ypsilanti. Since then, we haven't seen much of them. About three weeks ago, though, Fred passed the house. Harry and I were sitting on the porch. He waved to us."

Carl, the brother of Harry and son of Bert, who had been a friend of Smith, felt anger. "If Fred, is it," said Carl, "he'll never be sent to jail. They'll never get him from Ann Arbor."

Carl added, "And I'd like to lead the lynching mob."

As part of their confessions, both Blackstone and Smith had named Frank Oliver as the third man. Two carloads of deputies, with Smith in one, stopped at a house on Pearl Street, where Oliver was employed painting. He was pulled off a ladder before he realized what was happening. The police returned to city hall.

Oliver had no criminal history. Those who knew him said he was wild and drank a good deal and went about with girls some. He was described as shiftless in his appearance, so the nicer girls did not go out with him. Someone who knew him said: "Frank Oliver was a very pleasant spoken boy, polite and well mannered. But he drank and smoked, as boys will. We never supposed he was vicious."

About ten years before, the Oliver family had lived on River Street. where Frank was said to be polite but a terror; he would destroy property in nearby yards. The neighbors were pleased when the family moved.

By this time, news of the confessions had spread though the city, and a crowd of nearly one thousand people had gathered outside city hall. As officers rushed Smith and Oliver through the crowd and into city hall, some in the crowd made an attempt to seize Oliver, during which his clothes were ripped. Officers managed to lead Oliver into the building. He made his confession soon after his arrival at city hall.

In city hall, Blackstone expressed fears the crowd would lynch him. He had reason to be concerned, as the crowd milled about on all sides of the building. At one point, the mob, led by three ringleaders, tried to storm the doors of city hall but was repulsed by the forty-five officials on duty. Chief Deputy Sheriff Archie R. Fraser of Wayne County had requested that four teams of deputies, eight men in each, be sent to the city hall in Ypsilanti. Then, just before 5:00 p.m., every deputy in Wayne County was summoned.

Officials made a plan by which the three suspects would be conveyed to the Washtenaw County Jail in Ann Arbor. A car was parked in the rear of the building with sirens shrieking, and a large part of the mob moved to the back of city hall. At the same time, the three prisoners, manacled together, were rushed down the steps of city hall to a car at the curb. At this, the crowd surged toward the three, yelling, "Lynch them—burn them at the stake." As the three were rushing through the mob, some bystanders tore the shirts off the accused's backs. Deputies beat off the attack with the butts of their revolvers, injuring more than twenty in the melee.

The three prisoners were pushed into the waiting car at the curb as three husky deputies jumped onto the running boards, still beating off the mob with the butts of their revolvers. The rest of the deputies hurried to other cars parked by the curb. Then, with sirens shrieking, the deputies, with their prisoners, set off for Ann Arbor. Members of the mob set off after the deputies in their own cars.

The Washtenaw County Courthouse from an 1887 photograph, where the trial of the three accused killers was held while a mob called for them to be lynched. *Used with permission of the Bentley Historical Library, from the Pictorial History of Ann Arbor collection.*

"Arrival of the prisoners at the Ann Arbor jail after all deputies from the Sheriff's department, and a number of Ann Arbor police and special officers had been called to Ypsilanti, was one of the most spectacular and exciting events of the day," noted the *Ypsilanti Daily Press* of Friday, August 14, 1931. The article continued:

> *Shrieking sirens could be heard as the cavalcade approached the jail and doors at both sides of the office were thrown open, no one on the inside knowing which way the cars would come.*
>
> *The stop was made at the Ann St. entrance and two deputies, with the prisoners handcuffed between them, made a dash for the front door. All the prisoners were frightened, as they were jerked through the door with a mob at their heels. Deputies who were with them shouted hoarsely for those inside the jail to unlock the cell block and raced in there, shutting the heavy iron door before any attempt was made to remove the cuffs.*
>
> *They were perspiring freely when they came out and their disheveled appearance bore testimony of the difficulties through which they had gone.*
>
> *David Gartman, deputy who came in with the first rush of men, received a serious injury to his leg when it was necessary to slam shut the heavy oak door at the entrance to the office, in order to keep the mob, which had been in the business district but a short time before, from entering. Those barred out pounded on the doors but were not admitted.*
>
> *A large number of reporters and officials surged into the tiny office as the prisoners were admitted.*

Within fifteen minutes of the arrival of the deputies and their prisoners, a crowd of 1,500 had assembled at the front and back of the jail. The Michigan State Police moved the crowd three feet back from the jail fence and building. Guards were posted around the building and at the entrances of the jail. Washtenaw County Sheriff Andres called for the mobilization of the American Legion, members of which had offered their services in whatever way they might be needed.

Kate Keller arrived at the county jail at about the same time as Smith, Blackstone and Oliver. She had been taken into custody for questioning. As Keller was taken into the private office of the sheriff, she held a green coat, which she used to completely cover her head. Once in the office, Keller removed the coat, but in an almost hysterical state, she refused to talk as long as reporters were in the room. Keller was released soon after and was driven

Michigan State Police officers escort Blackstone, Smith and Oliver out of the Ypsilanti City Hall after they confessed to the murders. They passed through a crowd calling for the three to be lynched. *Used with permission of the Ypsilanti Historical Society. Used with permission of Tribune Content Agency.*

back to Ypsilanti by two students, one the son of a deputy sheriff. The police, however, were not done with her.

At the jail, Smith, Blackstone and Oliver were arraigned before Justice of the Peace Jay H. Payne, each on four warrants on the charge of murder. All three pleaded guilty to the charges. As part of the arraignment, Smith told his story of the murder. As he spoke, cries of "Hang them!" and "We'll hang them!" from the mob surrounding the building could be heard. Smith said he, Blackstone and Oliver had been to a blind pig called Louie's Place near Milan that night. There they had some drinks.

"I guess we got drunk," admitted Smith.

Smith said they recalled there was a poker game in the area, but the place was dark when they arrived. Then someone—each said it was one of the others—remembered that petting parties were to be found at Tuttle Hill. A good place for a holdup, they knew, with small profit but little risk. Here they found the car with Harry Lore, Thomas Wheatley, Vivian Gold and Anna

Mae Harrison. Blocking the parked car so it could not be driven away, at least two of the three approached the car.

Blackstone said it was Smith and Oliver who walked to the parked car. "Then Curley got scared when he saw it was Lore and some friends. He used to live near Lore, and he thought Lore would recognize him. He pulled one of the girls out of the car and asked her if Lore had recognized him. She said no. She tried to run away." Blackstone said Smith fired four shots.

Blackstone was vague on what happened next. Lore and Wheatley were dead. He said the four bodies were placed in the car and Blackstone, Smith and Oliver drove around not sure what to do.

"One of the girls in the back seat started to groan," said Blackstone. "I picked up a wrench from the floor of the car and slugged her. Then we stopped the car and pounded all four of the kids with rocks to make sure they were dead."

Finally, they poured gasoline over the car and bodies and set it afire.

Oliver said it was he who stayed in the car as Smith and Blackstone approached the victims' car, not at Tuttle Hill, but some distance away. Blackstone, said Oliver, came back to the car and told him they had taken two dollars. Then, with Smith driving as Oliver and Blackstone held guns on the four in the back seat of Wheatley's car, they drove to Tuttle Hill where, Oliver said, Blackstone dragged Anna Mae Harrison out of the car and assaulted her. Then, said Oliver, Blackstone told Vivian Gold to get out of the car. "The other girl said she would rather die than get out, so Blackstone shot her," testified Oliver.

RUSH TO COURTHOUSE

A crowd of some two thousand people had assembled outside the jail within fifteen minutes of the arrival of the prisoners. Because of the menacing mood of the crowd, fears of a lynching prompted Washtenaw County Circuit Court Judge George W. Sample to order the three to stand trial that night. Judge Sample ordered the three perpetrators delivered to his courtroom at the county courthouse after the completion of the arraignment. Now law enforcement officers had to convey the three from the jail in safety to the courthouse. The officers' understood speed was necessary for success.

Soon after the conclusion of the arraignment, each of the prisoners was handcuffed to two deputies and led out of the jail. A tear gas bomb was tossed onto the sidewalk to disperse the crowd, and Smith and Oliver were rushed to a waiting car at the curb. By this time, the crowd had surged in around Blackstone and his escort, separating them from the others. As Blackstone and his escort retreated to the jail, the car with Smith and Oliver sped off. Inside the jail, the doors were locked, and once the crowd rushed to follow the car with Smith and Oliver, Blackstone was led out a door at the rear of the jail and placed in a car there.

The courthouse was a three-story red brick building trimmed in limestone with a seven-story clock tower rising from the center. On each corner was a smaller tower, and above each of the four entrances, one on each side, was a statue of the goddess of Justice. Blindfolded, to show impartiality, and holding the scales of justice, the statues symbolized the purpose of the courthouse to administer the law and see the rights of the accused were protected. Below the statues, on the grassy lawn that surrounded

Members of the Michigan National Guard stand with police on the Washtenaw County Courthouse steps to hold off a mob of some twenty thousand people determined to lynch the accused killers. *Photo provided by John Hilton of* The Ann Arbor Observer. *Used with permission of Tribune Content Agency.*

the building, was a growing crowd of those who wished to take the three prisoners to the court of Judge Lynch.

"Arrival of the prisoners at the courthouse brought a scene of wild excitement, with shrieking sirens of the police cars cutting through the deep throated cries of the mob which was even then gathering in alarming proportions," reported the *Ypsilanti Daily Press* of Friday, August 14, 1931.

A crowd of some ten to fifteen thousand people surrounded the building. The mob was kept at bay by twenty-five Michigan National Guardsmen standing on the steps of the courthouse holding rifles with fixed bayonets. At the rear of the building was a line of Michigan State Police officers, and on each side of the building stood a contingent of members of the American Legion. Smith and Oliver were delivered to the courthouse and rushed to the entrance; the mob tried to seize them as they passed through, ripping at their clothing.

Standing shoulder to shoulder, members of the Michigan National Guard and Wayne County sheriff deputies and Washtenaw County sheriff deputies held back the mob. *Photo provided by John Hilton of* The Ann Arbor Observer. *Used with permission of Tribune Content Agency.*

The prisoners were pushed or dragged through the crowd and entered the building, taken into the central lobby and then up one of the grand staircases to the second floor, where Judge Sample had his courtroom.

"Oliver," noted the *Ypsilanti Daily Press*, "was the first to arrive in the courtroom, shackled to two sturdy deputies, and giving evidence of having been literally dragged along by the men sworn to protect his life against the indignant populace. His shirt was torn to shreds at the back and had been ripped open to the waist in front." Oliver sank into a chair, still handcuffed, and slouched down in his seat, staring at the floor with his hair in his eyes.

Smith arrived next; the sleeves of his shirt had nearly been torn off, and the back of his shirt was in tatters. He was dressed in heavy overalls which had not been damaged during the struggle to pass through the mob. Standing beside Oliver, Smith looked stonily before him.

"For almost an hour about two hundred spectators, photographers, newspaper men and officers waited in the court room before Oliver and Smith were brought in," reported the *Ann Arbor Daily News* of August 14, 1931. "While Detective Sergeant Stanley Ferguson of the state police, Deputies William Daily, James Wanzeck and James Dunstone and two Wayne County deputies posed for camera men, police posted themselves at all doors of the building to prevent anyone from entering." Seated near the front of the court was Fielding H. Yost, legendary director of athletics at the University of Michigan.

"The courtroom, despite the disturbance outside, remained orderly. The court officer rapped a few times to stop the loud whispering, but despite the jam, there was no real disorder. Jury box and tables overflowed with more newspapermen and women than ever covered a football game in this college community," noted the *Detroit Free Press*.

The car carrying Blackstone arrived at the rear entrance to the courthouse. As Blackstone was rushed to the door, members of the mob moved in on him and his escort and tried to pull him away. In the courtroom, cries of "They've got him!" could be heard. Despite this, Blackstone soon appeared in the courtroom and took his place beside Oliver and Smith.

"The prisoners were a horrible trio," noted the *Detroit Free Press* of Friday, August 14, 1931. "Hair disheveled, shirts and clothing torn to shreds, in the case of Smith, a remnant eight inches square being all that was left of his coat, they gave mute evidence of the eagerness of the crowd to get them, both at the jail and the courthouse. Puffed faces, bruised lips told of blows that went home."

As the three waited for the proceedings to begin, they sat quietly, handcuffed to deputies, occasionally nodding or making a short reply to a question.

Photographers were allowed to take pictures of the three for fifteen minutes while everyone awaited the arrival of Judge George W. Sample. Judge Sample entered the courtroom at 7:00 p.m., and the proceeding of the court began at 7:05 p.m.

5

TRIAL

Albert Rapp, the prosecutor, began the proceedings by making a motion that the court appoint an attorney to represent the three, as they were jointly charged with murder. Judge Sample agreed and appointed attorney John Mellott to represent the three. The proceedings continued, with Mellott never holding a private meeting with his three clients.

"May it please the Court," said Rapp, "we have the case of the People of the State of Michigan vs. Fred Smith, David Blackstone and Frank Oliver charged with the murder of one Thomas Wheatley."

Judge Sample turned to the three defendants and said, "You understand with what you are charged and now that you are represented, desire that we proceed at this time?"

In turn, Smith, Blackstone and Oliver each answered, "Yes."

Judge Sample asked the three how they desired to plead to the charge.

Each in turn answered, "Guilty."

Then, in turn, Smith, Blackstone and Oliver were charged with the murder of Anna Mae Harrison, Vivian Gold and Harry Lore. Each time the three were asked how they desired to plead, and each time each answered, "Guilty."

Once the formal opening proceedings were completed, the first witness was called; this was Lynn Squires, Washtenaw County deputy sheriff.

Deputy Squires testified he was acquainted with Thomas Wheatley and had seen him on Monday evening at about eight o'clock. This was on Michigan Avenue in Ypsilanti.

"Where did you next see Mr. Wheatley?" asked Rapp.

"In the automobile on County Line Road," answered Squires.

"And what was the condition of Mr. Wheatley when you saw him next?" asked Rapp.

Squires answered, "He was dead, and his body had been burned."

"You could identify it as that of Thomas Wheatley?"

"It was hard to make an identification, but I decided it was him," said Squires. "The body was almost past identification."

"How did you?"

"By the size of the man and the little cloth left under the arm, and the belt buckle and keys left on him."

"That was after he was dead?"

"He was dead, yes."

"Were you present at the time he was identified by his parents?"

"I was not."

"That is all," said Rapp.

Mellott had no questions.

The next witness called was Fred Smith, who said he was willing to make a statement. He gave his testimony in a low, halting voice: "I was up to this place with this one boy, Frank Oliver and met David Blackstone there. We were up there and got disorderly on hooch. I didn't know what I was about. I went with the boys during this time, and we went up on the grove where these couples was. Up there David Blackstone suggested we go and stick them up. We did and these boys identified me and Frank Oliver. So, we took them up on Tuttle Hill Road."

Rapp asked, "What boys do you mean?"

"Harry Lore and Wheatley," answered Smith. "And took them there and in the scuffle, we shot them. David Blackstone had a gun, and he shot each one once and I ain't sure which ones he hit. I stood alongside of the car. I couldn't see which ones he hit. He shot while I stood there. We took them from there. We dragged them out of the car. They weren't quite dead. I threw a stone on Harry Lore's head. In the scuffle we threw them in the car and drove to the county road where we set fire to the auto. Then we took Frank Oliver's car and started toward Ypsilanti and went home. It was Monday night about 5:30 when we arrived in Ypsilanti. I guess that's all."

"You remember who set fire to the car?" asked Rapp.

"I put gasoline on the floorboards, and we started to drive away. One of the boys lit a match and throwed the match in the car while we drove by it."

"Which one?"

Aerial view of the Peninsular Paper Mill, 1935, on the south side of the Huron River. Across the river on the north side is Peninsular Grove, a well-known lover's lane. This is where Frank Oliver, Fred Smith and David Blackstone found the two couples. The two couples and their killers got in Wheatley's car, which was driven to the road, then across the bridge and over the river, then across the railroad tracks and over Railroad Street to briefly stop at the corner of Huron River Drive. Here the car was directly across the street from the home of Harry Lore. *Used with permission of the Ypsilanti Historical Society.*

"I don't know."

"Have you anything further to say?"

"No, that's all."

"So that the first time the shots were fired was in Peninsular Grove and not in Tuttle Hill."

"We held them up with a gun."

"A bullet was put in each one of them?"

"Four shots were fired. I don't know who was hit."

"After that they were all dead?"

"Two of them were."

"What two?"

"I don't know. One of the girls and Thomas Wheatley."

"Were the girls attacked?"

"I couldn't say for sure. I know I didn't."

"Did you have an argument with Vivian Gold?"

"No."

"After she recognized you?"

"No, she didn't recognize me. I didn't know her."

"After they were hit on the head with stones, they were loaded into the car?"

"Yes, we took them to the town line."

"Who was driving?"

"I did from Tuttle Hill and Frank drove his car."

"While you were driving from Tuttle Hill to Town Line Road, did any one of the victims come to?"

"One of the girls did."

"What happened to her?"

"I don't know for sure, but I think David hit her with a wrench."

"Wasn't she down under the other bodies?"

"No, in the front seat."

"With you?"

"She climbed over."

"Who else was in the car besides you and David Blackstone? He was in the car with you?"

"Yes, he was with me."

"At that time three were dead and one crawled over on the front seat?"

"They were not all dead."

"Which girl was it?"

"I don't know. I didn't know her."

"One was small and the other large?"

"They were both the same size to me."

"So, the actual murder took place on Tuttle Hill?"

"Yes."

At this, the testimony of Fred Smith ended, as there were no further questions. The next witness called was Washtenaw County Sheriff Jacob B. Andres.

Sheriff Andres was asked where Tuttle Hill is. He answered that it was one mile east and two miles south of Ypsilanti, in Washtenaw County in the state of Michigan. This placed the crime within the jurisdiction of the court.

"With the consent of the Court," said Rapp, "if the Court please, and with the consent of counsel for the respondents, I would like to have the testimony corpus collecti and as to the location at which the murder was committed."

"All right," said Judge Sample. "This testimony may be considered as applying to each of the respondents."

The next witness called to testify was Frank Oliver, who was duly sworn.

"You know," said Judge Sample, "that you are charged with the crime of murder, and you are not required to testify. If you wish to testify, you may but you are not compelled to do so. That is the law in the State of Michigan."

"I will testify," replied Oliver.

"Very well," answered Judge Sample.

Then, under the questioning of Rapp, Frank Oliver told his version of events of the night of Monday, August 11, 1931.

Oliver said he drove his car, a Pontiac coach, to the house of Otis Oden, to see Fred Smith. He said his only reason for going there was to see Fred Smith. He did admit to having one shot of whiskey while there, which was given to him by Otis Oden.

At the house, he found Smith and David Blackstone, and the two wanted him to take them for a ride in his car. Oliver said they went to Peninsular Grove at around 10:30 p.m. Peninsular Grove is at the north side of Ypsilanti, directly across the Huron River from the Peninsula Paper Mill. The grove had been the site of a second paper mill owned by the company until it was destroyed by fire in the late 1890s. By 1931, the grove had become a lovers' lane where petting parties were held.

"Why," asked Rapp, "did you go to Peninsular Grove?"

"We were going to go up and hold someone up and get some money. We were broke." This, said Oliver, was at the suggestion of David Blackstone.

At about midnight, they found only one car at the Grove, the one that belonged to Thomas Wheatley.

"We drove around the grove and back up there and Blackstone and Fred jumped out and went over to Tom Wheatley's car and left me in the automobile, in my car, and they went over there to the Wheatley car and held them up."

Oliver said he remained in his car while Smith and Blackstone held up the two couples.

"Then what did they do?" asked Rapp.

"They just monkeyed around and come over and said they were going to drive the other car. They were going to take them into the country so they wouldn't report them."

Then all of them got into the Wheatley car, with Fred Smith driving, Blackstone seated in the center of the front seat and Oliver on the right side of the front seat. Wheatley, Lore, Vivian Gold and Anna Mae Harrison were in the back seat. As Smith drove, Blackstone and Oliver held guns on the couples. As Smith was driving, he handed his gun to Oliver, who then held it on the couples in the back seat.

"Did you hear any conversation?" asked Rapp.

"No, sir," answered Oliver, "only they said, 'let us go and we won't report you.' Blackstone said, 'yes, and then we land in the jug.'"

Smith drove the car to Tuttle Hill and stopped next to the river. There Smith, Blackstone and Oliver got out of the car. Blackstone, said Oliver, ordered Anna Mae Harrison out of the car.

"Did he attack Miss Harrison?" asked Rapp.

"Yes sir."

"Where were you?"

"Standing next to the car."

"What were you doing?"

"Just standing there."

"Did you have the gun in your hand?"

"Yes, sir." Oliver continued, "Blackstone came over and was going to make Vivian Gold get out of the car. She said she would rather die than get out. He said 'die.' He shot her."

At this, a murmur rippled through the spectators in the courtroom.

"Where was she?"

"Sitting in the back seat. As soon as he shot her, he shot the other three. He shot four shots."

Because of her refusal to leave the car, Vivian Gold became known as the "girl who chose death before dishonor." The final report of the autopsy would not be released until the following Monday, and it would cast doubt on the account given by Oliver.

Blackstone then pulled the bodies out of the car and placed them on the ground.

"Were they dead?" asked Rapp.

"No sir, Lore got up to fight and Blackstone knocked him down."

"Did Smith hit any of them with a stone?"

"I didn't see it."

"Did you hear Fred testify?"

"Yes, sir."

"Where were the girls?"

"Lying on the ground."

"All of the bodies were out of the car?"

"Yes, sir."

"Then what did you do?"

"After they were killed with the stone, Smith threw the stone in the river."

"They crushed the girls heads with the stone?"

"No, sir," said Oliver. "The girls were not hit with the stone."

"How were they killed?"

"One was shot with a bullet and the other was beaten with a wrench."

"Who beat her with a wrench?"

"Blackstone."

"Did he shoot her at all?"

"He shot four shots; I don't know who he hit."

"Why did you lay the bodies on the ground?"

"We were going to go back after my car."

"You were going to leave them there?"

"Yes, sir."

"Why didn't you?"

"We were afraid they would be discovered sooner."

The bodies were placed back in Wheatley's car.

"Did you pick them up and throw them?"

"No, we laid them in carefully."

Then, with the four bodies in the car, the three drove back to Peninsular Grove and Oliver's car. There, Oliver got in his car and followed Smith and Blackstone as they drove out of Peninsular Grove on to what is today LeForge Road. Under the questioning of Rapp, Oliver told the court of what happened next.

Oliver said he followed Smith and Blackstone across the railroad tracks. At the corner of LeForge Road and Huron River, the two cars were almost directly across the street from the Lore home—the place where only hours before, the two couples had set out for the evening. Then they turned onto the River Road, now Huron River Drive.

"How far did you go on that?"

"I don't know. Down to where the road cuts across and goes to Packard Road."

"Is that road open?"

"No, sir."

"What did you do?"

"We went down it."

"Isn't it covered with fresh tar?"

"It had been on about a day."

They continued on that road to the top of the hill east of the Washtenaw Country Club.

"Then where did you go?"

"We turned right and went to Michigan Avenue and turned to the left up to First Street, up by the dairy. Blackstone went and got a shovel."

"Where?"

"I don't know. He swiped it."

"What did you want it for?"

"To bury them."

"Where did you go after you got the shovel?"

"I got gas and went out Michigan."

Oliver said he stopped at a gas station on Michigan Avenue, next to a miniature golf course by the dairy. This was at 2:00 a.m.

"You stopped there at the gas station with the four dead bodies?"

"No, sir, I had my car."

"Where was the other car?

"Ahead."

"You were following them."

"Yes, I was afraid to leave them and afraid to go with them."

Oliver continued to follow Smith and Blackstone as they drove around. They stopped at an old gravel pit. There they considered burying the bodies. They chose not to do so, as Blackstone thought it would take too long.

"Where did you go?"

"We went out on the country road where they were burned."

"Just what happened?"

"We all stopped there, and they pulled up on the right and I on the left next to them while Fred and I got some gas out of the Wheatley car."

Smith removed the top of the tank with Oliver's pliers. Then he used a tin can they had found at the gravel pit to carry the gasoline to the Wheatley car. There he poured the gasoline over the cushions and floorboards of the car, but not on the bodies.

"Who set fire to it?"

"Blackstone."

After the fire was set, Smith turned Oliver's car around and Oliver jumped in.

"Where did you go?"

"We came back to Ypsilanti."

"Where did you go then?"

"They went home, and I went home."

Under further questioning by Rapp, Oliver said Blackstone took the body of Anna Mae Harrison out of the car and carried her to the ditch. There he assaulted her for a second time. Then he placed the body in the car.

"Where were you at that time?"

"I was standing with my back to the car."

"Where was Smith?"

"With me."

"Did Smith attack anyone?"

"No, sir."

"Did you?"

"No, sir."

Judge Sample asked, "Is there any further testimony?"

In answer to this question Rapp said, "I do not care to take any further testimony."

STATEMENT OF JUDGE SAMPLE

"The Court," pronounced Judge Sample, "finds under the testimony as produced in open court, in the first place, Thomas G. Wheatley met his death by being murdered and murder being first degree murder, by respondents Fred Smith, David Blackstone and Frank Oliver. The Court finds further in the case of the People versus the three respondents mentioned heretofore that Anna Mae Harrison came to her death by being murdered and murder being first degree murder by respondents Fred Smith, David Blackstone, and Frank Oliver. And the Court finds further in the next case that Vivian Gold was murdered and that the murder was first degree and committed by Fred Smith, David Blackstone and Frank Oliver and the Court further finds in the other case, the last case, that Harry Lore was murdered, the murder being first degree murder and that his death was caused by being murdered by Fred Smith, David Blackstone, and Frank Oliver.

"The Court finds these murders were committed within the County of Washtenaw on the morning of August 11, 1931.

"The Court," added Judge Sample, "desires to interview each of the respondents privately."

Judge Sample then adjourned the proceedings and retired to his chambers to meet privately with Smith, Blackstone and Oliver. Present at the meeting were Prosecutor Rapp and Defense Attorney Mellott. No transcript of the meeting was recorded. During the meeting, it was later reported, Blackstone told Judge Sample that Smith and Oliver were trying to shift their guilt onto him. The meeting concluded after thirty minutes, after which Judge Sample, Rapp, Mellott, Smith, Blackstone and Oliver returned to the courtroom.

When proceedings resumed, Prosecutor Rapp spoke. "May it please the Court," said Rapp, "we have the case of the People of the State of Michigan vs. Frank Oliver, Fred Smith and David Blackstone for sentence."

Judge Sample asked if there was any reason why judgment should not be given.

Defense Attorney Mellott asked the court to consider the age and testimony of Oliver, "and after listening to the testimony, he kindly exercise what leniency the case may call for."

"I ask," said Judge Sample, "if any of you have anything to say as to why judgment should not be pronounced against you in any of these cases? Has the Prosecuting Attorney anything to say?"

At this, Blackstone said, "They came to my place and got me."

Then Prosecutor Rapp spoke: "May it please the court, as between the respondents, they are all equally guilty in the eyes of the law in whatever part they participated in the most atrocious crime ever committed in the State of Michigan, if not within the United States. I think that under the circumstances I could not ask leniency of this Court and it would certainly be the recommendation of the Prosecutor's office that they be given the full penalty to the full extent of the law."

The full penalty under the laws of Michigan was life imprisonment. The State of Michigan had abolished the death penalty for the crime of murder in 1848, the first government in the Western world to do so.

Rapp, continuing his statement to the court, then thanked the officers of the court and law for their work in solving the crime. "Everyone," said Rapp, "worked together harmoniously toward one goal, to bring into custody the men who committed such a terrible crime as was committed in our county August 11th. Everyone worked together and that cooperation brought about the quick apprehension."

Then Judge Sample asked, "Has defense anything to say?"

"No, your honor," answered Mellott. "I am only desirous of making certain Mr. Blackstone who has no one, tell his story to you in a way you desired to hear it."

"I think," said Judge Sample, "Mr. Blackstone was given an opportunity." Judge Sample continued with his concluding statement.

> *If I were to express my feelings on this occasion, I feel I would be compelled to say as to these three persons in human form that I feel like I am in the presence of fiends. I don't wonder that the crowd is howling for vengeance. If they had listened to this testimony, that we have had to listen to give these parties their rights under the laws of the state, I am afraid they would not be as civil as they are.*
>
> *There is a law of civilization that we must not indulge the law. The law must take its course. The people of the state of Michigan have declared that the penalty for this crime is life imprisonment.*
>
> *We all know that it doesn't make the penalty severe enough in this case. But if the law as it is administered promptly and properly that is all that we can ask. We are here to administer the law as it is and all good citizens will abide by it. How human beings could act as you three have acted goes beyond me. I can't imagine it. The testimony made me heartsick—that our highways and our places of pleasure should have to be infested by such worms.*
>
> *Society has no place for them, it never can. If they should live 1,000 years, they would not be fit to come back. I put them all on an equal basis. There might be something to say for Frank Oliver—but he associated himself with these men. Sometimes I feel discouraged. This young man Smith has been before me before for years and prominent citizens of Ypsilanti have tried to do something for him to show him what was right and wrong. Supervisors and other good citizens have tried to lead him aright and I can't help believe that if it wasn't for him, this crime would not have been committed.*
>
> *The others should not be misled by that statement. They are old enough and know enough to know better. I do not think it is necessary for me to say anything further and I proceed to the sentence.*

As Judge Sample began to pronounce sentence on each of the three, the clock above his head read 8:56 p.m.

"It is the judgment of the court," said Judge Sample, "and it is so ordered that these three respondents in each of four cases for the murder of each of the four persons be committed to that branch of the Michigan state prison known as the Marquette branch for and during their natural lives in each case, and the sentences are not to run concurrently. The court wants to make doubly sure that they are never again to menace society. The sheriff's department is authorized to remove them to Jackson prison until they can be removed to Marquette."

The sentencing of each of the three to four consecutive life terms may have been the harshest penalties ever dealt out in the history of the state of Michigan.

"I want to commend the sheriff, Mr. Harry Bennett and his men, the state police and the others—I want to commend you all for bringing to justice three fiends in human form so quickly."

RUSH FROM COURTHOUSE

After legal proceedings had been concluded, everyone in the courtroom was ordered to remain where they were, except children seated in the windows. Officials were concerned the children would shout information to the mob below when the prisoners were removed. Officials reconsidered keeping the spectators in the courtroom and decided it was best if they left. The spectators were then told they could leave. The courthouse building was now cleared of everyone but officers, newspapermen and photographers. Smith, Oliver and Blackstone remained in the courtroom.

Now with the trial over, Smith, Blackstone and Oliver sat in the courtroom waiting for events to play out. The three were perhaps relieved the ordeal was coming to an end. They were exhausted from the long hours of questioning. The three were willing to talk about the case with anyone who was willing to listen. They seemed to enjoy being in the limelight. They said they were sorry but showed no deep feeling of emotion or regret over what they had done.

As the mob surrounding the courthouse shouted, "Lynch them!" Mill Marsh, sportswriter for the *Ann Arbor Daily News*, briefly interviewed the three. The paper published his story on Friday, August 14, 1931.

"I would rather be lynched than sent to prison," said Blackstone. "In fact, any kind of death would be welcome. I'm just beginning to realize what a hideous crime I committed. There is nothing that anybody could do to me that I don't deserve. Just so I die is all I care."

Frank Oliver said he "was sorry and had been ever since the crime was committed. I knew that it was only a question of time before the officers would get me. I haven't eaten or slept since that night. Why I did it I don't

The three killers on display for press photographers with Frank Oliver on the left, handcuffed to Fred Smith dressed in overalls, and David Blackstone, in a dark suit, after having been sentenced to four consecutive life terms. *Used with permission of Tribune Content Agency.*

know. It's going to be tough on my four sisters and three brothers. I followed the case in the papers and was not surprised to see the officers coming for me. I deserve what I am getting. I never thought of running away."

"I guess that I've always been wild," said Fred Smith as he fumbled a fifty-cent piece, his share of the loot from the robbery, "and I wanted to stick up somebody just for a thrill. I never realized that it would come to this. I have nobody but myself to blame. I went into this crime on my own free will and accord."

All through the trial, the size of the mob had grown until it may have numbered some ten thousand people, who had come from miles around. The crowd overflowed the courthouse lawn and filled the surrounding streets. From time to time, a false sighting of the prisoners caused the mob to rush from one end of the building to the other.

"For time, uniformed police and the newly organized Military police patrolled the scene with night sticks and riot guns plainly displayed, but only in one or two instances where police forced to emphasize orders with night stick taps," noted the *Ann Arbor News.*

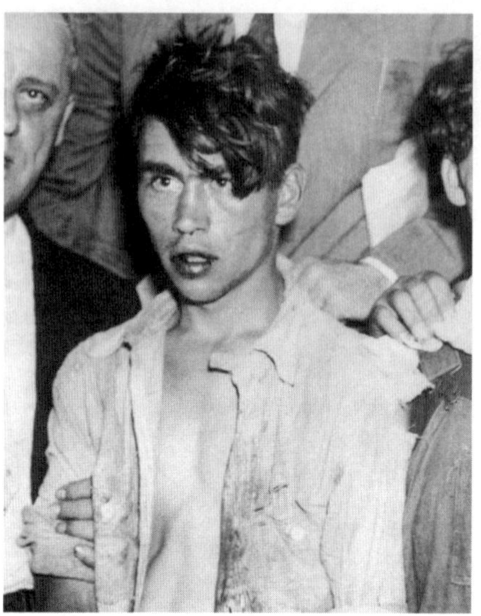

Frank Oliver stands before reporters and photographers after the trial, nose bloody, lip swollen, as he appears dazed, while surrounded by police and procurators. *Photo provided by John Hilton of* The Ann Arbor Observer. *Used with permission of Tribune Content Agency.*

"State Rep. Phil C. Pack, of Ann Arbor, had wired Gov. Brucker to send two companies of guardsmen from Jackson to Ann Arbor," reported the *Detroit News* of Friday, August 14, 1931. "The Governor refused on the ground such a request must come from the sheriff. Sheriff Andres said he did not believe the presence of more soldiers to be necessary and declined to make the request."

A plan was made to get the three out of the building by turning off the lights of the courthouse. The three were handcuffed to deputies and led to the top of the stairs and started down. The lights in the lobby of the building were turned off.

At this, someone in the mob yelled, "They're coming!"

A roar rose from the mob.

The deputies and prisoners were halfway down the winding and creaking staircase when the procession stopped and then turned back up the stairs and returned to the courtroom. "Grimy with sweat," noted the *Detroit Free Press*, "with their clothes torn, their hands and arms dirty, their shirt tails hanging out Oliver and Smith looked pathetic. Blackstone showed fright."

To try to calm the mob, Rapp stepped out of the courthouse and onto the steps in front of the building. He stood with the members of the National Guard, who held their rifles with fixed bayonets.

"Please," said Rapp, "this is one time you must help us. We know what these boys deserve. We know what ought to be done with them, but we must throw that out of our minds.

"We are law abiding citizens. I am your neighbor, and I am appealing to you to abide by the law of Michigan. It is our duty to see that these men are carried safely to jail. These men will not be the ones to get hurt if you attempt to do anything. The ones to get hurt will your officers, men who reside in your community and try to protect your interests and rights.

"It is their job to protect these men from you. Suppose some of you are hurt. What good will that do? Suppose one of the officers are hurt. That will not help in any way. There has been enough bloodshed. Let us forget these men and do justice as the law of Michigan provides."

His words seemed to have influenced the crowd, but as soon as Rapp turned his back, one man in the crowd cried out, "Bring them out." The words of Rapp were forgotten.

Back in the courtroom, officers held a meeting to work out a new plan to get the three to the prison at Jackson. Harry Bennett of the Ford Motor Company urged haste, as the crowd outside was growing, and further delay, he feared, would only increase the danger. As the men talked, a new plan was worked out.

At 10:30 p.m., sixty deputies gathered around Smith, Oliver and Blackstone. Some of the deputies handcuffed themselves to the three and prepared to rush out of the building. One deputy had sneaked out of the east end of the courthouse. Outside the building, he shouted, "Here they come."

At this, members of the crowd at other sides of the building rushed to the east end. At the same time, deputies at the north end of the building hurled tear gas bombs into the crowd in front of them. The tear gas caused the several hundred men who had stayed at the north end to move away from the building.

By now, Harry Bennett had parked his car on the sidewalk in front of the courthouse, with one rear wheel on the courthouse steps. The deputies and the prisoners now made a rush to the car. Someone threw a brick at Blackstone, but the aim was bad, and the brick hit the courthouse. Smith, Oliver and Blackstone, still handcuffed to deputies and each other, were pushed into the rear seat of the car. Officers, their guns leveled, cleared a pathway through the crowd as the car cut across the lawn, between trees and over the curb. They had made a clean getaway.

The prisoners were five blocks away from the courthouse when the escort caught up with them. On West Huron Street, a procession formed with a Michigan State Police car, packed with armed men, in the lead. This was followed by Bennett's car, which was followed by another Michigan State

Police car. Other cars were strung out behind them. Cars in pursuit of the procession tried to catch up but soon dropped out.

"Tacks discovered on the route which it had been planned to take," reported the *Ypsilanti Daily Press*, "led to abandonment of the first plan and the car went by way of Saline after circling Ann Arbor."

The forty-mile trip to Jackson was completed in one hour. "All during the hour's ride the prisoners stared at the passing scenery and kept silent, except when Mr. Bennett asked them whether they would prefer to be at liberty or in prison. Blackstone replied that he would rather be in prison," reported the *Detroit Free Press*.

Word of the imminent arrival of the three had spread rapidly through the community of Jackson, and a crowd of three thousand people had gathered at the gates to the prison. As a result, all available state and local police were stationed at the prison to clear the roads. Although the crowd appeared to be only curious, the three hundred police present fired tear gas to clear the way to the gates. The three convicts were escorted from the car and within two minutes were within the prison.

There the three were turned over to Prison Warden Harry H. Jackson. He gave them a grim welcome: "You needn't expect any favors here."

The three were then taken to the detention block, where they were placed in solitary confinement and on a diet of bread and water.

Early that evening, when word of the confession reached the home of Frank Oliver, his father tried to see his son. A newspaperman had driven him to the courthouse, but because of the crowd and the lines of police, they were unable to reach the building. For two hours, the father sat in the car as the trial proceeded and the crowd around them yelled for the three to be lynched.

At last, he was informed of the conclusion of the trial.

"Did the trial show that Frank had any part in the actual killing?" he asked.

"No!" he was told.

"Thank God for that!" he said. Then he burst into tears.

The investigation was not over, as there were many questions that still needed to be answered. The authorities wanted to know if Smith, Oliver, and Blackstone had committed other crimes, the cases of which could now be closed. Another question the police wanted to answer was if others were involved in the murder.

Even as Smith, Oliver and Blackstone were being delivered to Jackson Prison, police were placing Kate Keller under arrest as a possible accomplice after the fact to the murders.

FRIDAY, AUGUST 14, 1931

As Smith, Oliver and Blackstone were being delivered to Jackson Prison, Washtenaw County Deputy Sheriff William F. Dailey and Detective Lieutenant N.R. Black were at 407 Campbell Avenue in Ypsilanti, the residence of Kate Keller, the "sweetheart" of Smith. There the officers found clothing belonging to Smith in a cedar chest. At the request of the officers, Keller produced a .32-caliber revolver believed to have been carried by Smith during the crimes. A number of blood-spattered newspapers were found in the furnace of the house. Whoever placed the papers in the furnace had forgotten to set fire to them.

Keller was taken into custody for further questioning and conveyed to the county jail in Ann Arbor. There she was questioned by Prosecutor Rapp between 2:00 and 3:00 a.m. She told Rapp the revolver had belonged to her uncle, the late Judge Darwin Z. Curtiss, who had died in February of that year. She said she had loaned the gun to Smith several times, and he had always returned it.

She explained she had come to know Smith through her uncle, who was known to sometimes take a kindly interest in some of those who came before him. Keller said she felt sorry for Smith when he was released from prison and loaned him money while he was unemployed. Smith, she said, had proposed to her the week before the murders, but she had delayed giving him an answer.

She admitted to having been with the three on Monday evening at Oden's place, but, because she had a date that evening, she said, they dropped her off at her place at about 9:00 p.m. before driving to Peninsular Grove.

Rapp planned to travel to Jackson Prison that day for further questioning of Smith, Oliver and Blackstone. The role of Kate Keller was one of the topics he wanted to ask them about.

As Rapp made his way to Jackson Prison, Deputy Sheriff Lynn Squires was making his way out to Tuttle Hill to look for the site of the murders. As he searched, Squires found a lane that wound down to the Huron River, about a half mile from where Vivian Gold's purse had been found. Following the lane down, he found a site by the river covered with blood with blood-spattered stones, trampled grass and broken bushes.

"It looked as if the slaughter of a herd of animals had occurred there," said Squires.

At the site, he found Anna Mae Harrison's coin purse, containing eighty-nine cents, and an earring. A second search of the site on Saturday turned up Anna Mae Harrison's handbag, which was covered with blood. The handbag contained blood-stained scraps of paper, a restaurant napkin and three earrings.

This was not the only search of the area that was being carried out. There was the question of possible other crimes the three may have committed. Some recent events were deemed worthy of a second look. On the morning of August 6, a stolen Chrysler five-passenger sedan was found burning on Harris Road, near Tuttle Hill, three hundred feet from the Huron River. A second car had been seen leaving the site not long before.

Members of the Detroit Police Department and members of the Ypsilanti Police Department carried out a search of the Huron River near the murder site to determine if other murders may have been committed there. The search turned up no evidence of any other victims of murder. *Used with permission of Tribune Content Agency.*

On Friday, August 14, under the direction of Patrolman Coy Rankin, law enforcement dragged the river near the site where the car had been found. This was done to determine if another murder had been committed and the body disposed of in the river. The operation was discontinued at nightfall, with no bodies recovered. Police concluded the stolen burned car was not linked to any other crimes.

As Squires conducted his search of the site of the murder, at about 2:00 p.m., Prosecutor Rapp and Assistant Attorney General Edward A. Bililzke arrived at the prison in Jackson to continue the questioning of Smith, Oliver and Blackstone.

Just after Rapp and Bililzke arrived at the prison, the family of Oliver arrived as well. Oliver's father, mother, brother and sister-in-law were permitted to visit. The parents clasped their arms around him, and with tears streaming down their faces, they professed their faith in his innocence.

When Smith, Oliver and Blackstone were questioned on Thursday, before the trial, each seemed to imply that Kate Keller had been with them during the holdup at Peninsular Grove and possibly during the murders at Tuttle Hill. This time, as Rapp and Bililzke questioned them, Smith, Oliver and Blackstone each said Keller had been with them early on Monday evening, at Oden's place, but had left them at about 9:00 p.m. to go on a date. All three now said Keller had not been with them when the holdup and murders were committed.

Another line of questioning was to determine if Smith, Oliver and Blackstone were part of a gang that had been preying on "petting parties" over the previous months. In one such holdup, a young woman had been assaulted.

After eight hours of questioning, Rapp said he had made "a little progress."

"When Rapp left the killer last night," reported the *Ypsilanti Daily Press* of Saturday, August 15, 1931, "he was near collapse from overwork on the case."

Weary as he was, Rapp planned to return the next day, Saturday, to continue questioning of the three.

After Rapp and Bililzke had finished questioning the three, Smith received a visit from his father and mother. His mother, who was blind, ran her hands over his face as she greeted him. She placed the blame for his plight on Kate Keller. "She took you to blind pigs and kept you out nights," she said, sobbing. "If you had let her alone you would not be where you are."

Reportedly, Fred Smith was hardly moved. "The next time you see me," he said as they parted, "I'll be in a box."

The family of Fred Smith visited him after his arrival at Jackson Prison. He sits with his father and his mother, who was blind. The last thing he said to them before they returned home was, "The next time you see me, I'll be in a box." *Photo provided by John Hilton of* The Ann Arbor Observer. *Used with permission of Tribune Content Agency.*

Sometime on the evening of Friday, August 14, 1931, Judge Sample and assistant Washtenaw County prosecutor Carl A. Lehman ordered the arrest of Otis Oden for violation of probation. As Sample had questioned Smith, Oliver and Blackstone the night before about the murders, they had implicated Oden, as the series of events leading up to the murders had started with Oden selling them whiskey at his home. Oden, at the time, was under five years' probation, set by Judge Sample.

Late that evening, Washtenaw County Sheriff Deputies William Dailey, Floyd Hamacher and Clyde Bennett drove to Ypsilanti and immediately went to Oden's house. As the men made their way across the yard, they saw an African American man run from the house. The man collided with Deputy Bennett, throwing Bennett against a parked car and injuring Bennett's leg.

As the man ran toward a nearby field, Deputy Hamacher ordered the man to halt. As the man continued to run, Hamacher fired two shots from his gun and then captured the man. The man turned out to be George Elms, the man who had turned in the gun used by Blackstone. Elms later explained he had seen the men in the yard, and believing them to be friends of Smith seeking revenge, he fled. Elms was later released.

As Elms fled, Deputy Dailey had entered the house and begun a search. As Dailey was conducting his search, Ypsilanti Chief of Police Ralph Southard walked in. Southard demanded an explanation about what the deputies were doing in Ypsilanti and the reason for the shooting. Southard told Dailey; he could run his own town. Dailey later said, Southard's remarks were extremely "harsh."

When told the deputies had come in search of Oden, Southard said, "We got him two hours ago." Southard told them Oden had been arrested as he was leaving to go to Warren, Montana, on a charge of violating the prohibition act and was being held in the city jail.

Southard said he was a little surprised when he received a report of a shooting at the Oden place, as there was an understanding between the sheriff, the prosecutor and himself concerning raids without informing one another.

Judge Sample was not pleased with Southard's attitude, as the deputies were acting under his orders. Oden was to be arrested for breaking his probation, and under the terms of the probationary order, officers had the right to search Oden's premises at any time.

SATURDAY, AUGUST 15, 1931

The bodies of the victims were released to the families on Friday, August 14, and the remains of Vivian Gold and Anna Mae Harrison were returned to Cleveland that night. Funeral services for the two were held Saturday morning. The services were private and held separately at each of the family homes. This was followed by a joint service held at the Third United Brethren Church, where the two had been active members for several years. After the service, the remains of Vivian Gold were interred at Knollwood Cemetery, and those of Anna Mae Harrison were interred at White Haven Cemetery.

The funeral of Thomas Wheatley was held at the family home in Denton at 1:00 p.m. After the service, his body was buried at Sheldon Cemetery. The service for Harry Lore was held at 3:30 p.m. at the J.E. Moore funeral home in Ypsilanti. His body was buried at Highland Cemetery in Ypsilanti.

Above: Hundreds of people watch as the casket of Anna Mae Harrison is carried into the church in Cleveland. *Photo provided by John Hilton of* The Ann Arbor Observer. *Used with permission of Tribune Content Agency.*

Opposite, top: Remains of Harry Lore are carried to his grave in Highland Cemetery by members of the DeMolay Society, of which he and Thomas Wheatley were members. *From the* Detroit Daily Mirror *of Monday, August 17, 1931. Used with permission of Tribune Content Agency.*

Opposite, bottom: Family and friends bid goodbye to Thomas Wheatley at the site of his grave in Sheldon cemetery. *From the* Detroit Daily Mirror *of Monday, August 17, 1931. Used with permission of Tribune Content Agency.*

The services were attended by family and friends, without a gathering of the curious present. Members of the DeMolay, of which each was a member, served as pallbearers and honor guards.

The fact that the series of events that culminated in the murder and burning of the bodies of the four began in a blind pig led to a sense of revulsion against such establishments spreading through the population of Michigan. On the day of the funerals for the victims, Michigan Governor Wilbur Bruckner issued a statement calling on the law enforcement agencies of the state to wipe out these "cesspools of vice" that caused such crimes.

"I have requested Commissioner Oscar G. Olander, of the department of public safety, to clean up the state of Michigan, in co-operation with local authorities, to the end that youths will no longer be able to purchase moonshine and other poisonous whiskies that drive them to commit murder. I am asking all sheriffs and other law enforcement agencies to work hand-in-hand with us in this necessary clean-up," stated Governor Brucker.

"These youthful murderers," continued Brucker, "were under the influence of moonshine when they perpetrated this horrible crime. They had gone out to rob and kill to obtain more money for intoxicants. The fact that the youth of Michigan can obtain poisonous liquors in almost any part of the state is, in my opinion, largely responsible for the present wave of crime

"I am told there are thousands of resorts outside the boundaries of our cities where poisonous moonshine and liquors, made from raw alcohol, are sold almost openly.

"These resorts are on the borderline of all crime. They pander to our young folks and act as rendezvous. They are in a large measure responsible for our congested prisons and the crime wave that is a challenge to the state.

"These murders, probably the worst crime in Michigan history, must drive home to the enforcement officers the fact that vigorous prosecutions and determined warfare against the whiskey-selling joints are necessary at once. They must be closed and kept closed. The time has come for action.

"The state police are not to enter this drive alone. We do not want to send our clean-up into the counties uninvited. We want to co-operate, to work hand-in-hand with the various enforcement agencies in the hope that our united efforts will return Michigan to a day when moonshine crazed youths will not raid our homes and automobiles to rob and kill for money for liquor."

Oscar G. Olander, the commissioner of public safety, soon after called on the sheriffs of the eighty-three counties of the state to cooperate in a crackdown on the makers and sellers of bootleg liquor.

"This is not a question of prohibition enforcement," stated Olander. "It is a question of crime prevention by attacking the source. Only by exterminating these cesspools can our citizens be assured of personal safety on our highways and our city streets."

"Moonshine was responsible for these crimes and others," he noted. "The stuff makes maniacs of those who drink it and the sad part of it is that young boys and girls are addicts, partly because moonshine is cheap and plentiful."

Olander had sent instructions to the nineteen state police posts in the state to raid those places known to sell liquor without warrants. "We can make no arrests in such raids," he said, "but we can destroy the liquor and equipment and drive them out of business. There are moonshine addicts on the highways robbing and committing statutory offenses almost nightly. Their victims, luckily, are not always killed."

That evening, a number of blind pigs and speakeasies were raided by police, all within a three-mile radius of where the bodies had been found. Wayne County sheriff deputies carried out raids on their side of County-Line Road, and members of the Michigan State Police carried out raids on the Washtenaw County side of the road. These places were said to cater to students at the University of Michigan and the Michigan State Normal College, now Eastern Michigan University. Fred Smith, David Blackstone and Frank Oliver were said to frequent many of these farmhouse speakeasies.

The first place raided by the deputies was in the village of Martinville, directly across the street from the village church and school.

"[At] all of the farms visited," reported the *Ann Arbor Tribune* of Monday, August 17, 1931, "the owners appeared to have been warned and had hidden the liquor. The raiders found beer, whiskey and wine stored away in cornfields, hen coops, wells and haystacks. From several haystacks, upon which the sun beat all day, they pulled ice-cold bottles of beer, indicating that the contraband had recently been from a cold place and concealed in anticipation of the raid."

At a place on Rural Route 4 and John Karr Road, officers were told of a planned holdup, to have been carried out by Blackstone and Oliver, on the Friday before the murders. "They came to my place at night," said Louis Foder, "Blackstone carried a pistol and Oliver a flashlight. They said they were going to hold up my guests and started down to the basement where all the people were. But when they saw the crowd, I guess they lost their nerve because they didn't go in."

The following night, officers were told Smith and Oliver visited the Golden Dollar, a mile east of Martinville.

Officers raided the farm of Pauline Winicki, known as Annie Kluse, near Sumpter and Willis Roads.

"After resisting the officers," noted the account, "Mrs. Winicki told them about a secret chamber in Foder's basement and the raiders uncovered a large supply of liquor there, after breaking through a trap door."

"Foder," the account continued, "retaliated by telling of hiding places on Mrs. Winicki's farm, which deputies had overlooked, but by the time the information was obtained it was too dark to begin a new search."

As a result of the raids, deputies arrested five men and three women, confiscating 153 cases of beer and 6 barrels of whiskey.

"Since early Tuesday morning," reported the *Ann Arbor News* of Monday, August 17, "when the victim's blazing car was seen by a farmer on the County Line Road, thousands of persons have visited the spot. Sunday several hundred automobiles were parked in the vicinity while hundreds of the curious roamed over the ground where the clews were discovered."

Dr. John C. Bugher of the pathology department of the University of Michigan submitted his final report on the autopsy to Washtenaw County Coroner Gazhorn on the morning of Monday, August 17. The condition of the respiratory organs of Vivian Gold and Anna Mae Harrison proved the two were alive, but most likely unconscious, when the Wheatley car was set on fire.

The autopsy further determined that both Vivian Gold and Anna Mae Harrison had been sexually assaulted. This proved the trial testimony of Smith and Oliver, that Blackstone had assaulted only Harrison, was false. The technology did not then exist to determine if the two were assaulted by Blackstone, Smith or Oliver.

The Ypsilanti City Council held a meeting that evening, at which a resolution was passed giving thanks to and expressing confidence in the law enforcement agencies for the apprehension and conviction of the murderers. The council passed a second resolution, to have the city clerk express the sympathy of the city to the bereaved families of the victims.

Chief of Police Southard told the council he had the situation concerning blind pigs in the city well in hand. "In the opinion of Chief Southard," noted the *Ypsilanti Daily Press* of Tuesday, August 18, "there are not more than 15 actually menacing characters in the city, few blind pigs and no distilleries. Transient fugitives from justice and criminals who may have been loitering here, are expected to leave of their own accord following the wave of indignation aroused by the torch murders."

When asked by council about cleaning up the unsavory conditions in the city, he said he would use a "fine tooth comb" on the section of the where, he said, "stragglers and criminals are most apt to gather."

That same evening, Chief Southard led raids on five houses in the first ward of the city. These raids were carried out between 9:30 p.m. and midnight. At one house, a gallon jug of liquor and several empty bottles were found. The owner was arrested and charged with violation of the prohibition law. No liquor was found at the other four houses. The operators at these houses were told they were being watched, and their businesses would be closed if caught.

The trouble, county officials said, was to be found in western Wayne County, with Sumpter Township as the center of the liquor trade.

Police believed Smith, Blackstone and possibly Oliver were to blame for other crimes committed in southeast Michigan. Witnesses and victims of recent robberies and assaults traveled to the prison at Jackson to try to identify them as their assailants. None of these victims was able to identify any of the three as those who had carried out the crimes committed on them.

Fred Smith had, under questioning by Lynn Squires, said he had tossed a gun he had carried on the night of the murders into the Huron River, after it had jammed when he tried to shoot one of the four. He told Squires he had tossed the gun into the river, near the scene of the murders on Tuttle Hill. Squires was inclined to believe Smith, as a purse and a stone used in killing one of the girls was found where he had directed.

To carry out the search for the gun, Deputy Squires asked Harry Bennett, who had been a deep-sea diver in the navy, to help. Bennett agreed, and that afternoon, encased in a heavy rubber suit, steel helmet and metal shoes, he entered the waters at the site. The long air hoses stretched out from the helmet as he went under the water. The river at this point was twelve to fifteen feet deep. Bennett searched the river bottom for two hours.

"I can understand now why there have been so many drownings here," said Bennett later. "The river along here is full of whirlpools and there is a strong undercurrent that no one but a very strong swimmer could possibly combat."

During the search, Bennett said, he stepped into a hole at least five feet deep and the current pushed him off his feet. This, he explained, is something that rarely happens to an expert diver.

The search failed to turn up the gun, which may have been covered over by sediment on the soft river bottom.

The following day, Wednesday, August 19, employees of the Ford Motor Company cleared several acres of land near the site as part of the search for the gun. The land, owned by the company, was cleared of every vestige of weeds, brush and trees. As the site was cleared, the weeds and brush were carefully examined. The search turned up a hat worn by one of the girls, badly stained with blood, the pocketbook of Harry Lore and a necktie.

Officers began to wonder if Smith, Oliver and Blackstone had anything to do with the death of Wilson Blisner, who was found dead near the scene of the murders, on the night of July 19. At the time, the death was ruled an accident. On the afternoon of July 19, Blisner, who was twenty-four years of age and lived at Willis, had taken a young lady friend to Belleville. His car was found overturned at the jog in Tuttle Hill Road at about midnight. The overturned car was found by Dr. David Robb, who lifted the body from the wreckage. Dr. Robb checked the billfold for identification and saw there was cash inside but did not count the amount. He replaced the billfold so everything would be in order for the coroner's investigation. Dr. Robb then left the scene of the accident for a nearby farmhouse, from where he informed the authorities of the accident. Police later learned Blisner had about forty dollars in cash on his person at the time of his death and had a set of valuable radio tools in his car. The cash and tools were missing when authorities arrived on the scene.

Now the authorities wondered if Blisner was murdered by robbers, his body thrown onto the ground and the car tipped over onto his body. Smith and Oliver were said to have visited the funeral home to view the body, although they were not known to be acquainted with him. The two were said to have been accompanied by a woman when they visited the funeral home.

In the end, the authorities decided Blisner died in an accident. The loss of the money and tools, the authorities decided, was best explained by someone coming by the site, after Dr. Robb had left, finding the money and tools and carrying them off, leaving the site before anyone else arrived.

Prosecutor Rapp was still trying to solve the mystery of how blood came to be on the clothing and clubs of Paul and Lawrence Keene, who were arrested as suspects the day the bodies were found. By this time, it was clear the two had nothing to do with the murders, but still, Rapp wanted to clear up the question of the blood-stained clothing. Rapp noted that something had happened, and he was determined to find out what. The two were still in the county jail. Paul had pleaded guilty to violating the prohibition law; Lawrence had demanded an examination and was being held in default of bail.

Paul Keene tried to kill himself by slashing his throat with a razor at about 8:30 p.m. on Wednesday, August 19. The attempt was almost immediately discovered by deputies, and after a struggle, he was taken to the hospital to recover.

"The elder Keene has been in a serious condition ever since being taken to jail. According to neighbors, both brothers have been in a state of semi-intoxication most of the time for the past few years, and in jail, Paul Keene has suffered several attacks of 'fits,'" reported the *Ypsilanti Daily Press* of Thursday, August 20, 1931.

The story of how the two came to have blood-stained clothing came out after the suicide attempt. "The two men," reported the *Ypsilanti Daily Press* of Friday, August 21, 1931, "intoxicated, quarreled over a drill which Paul accused Lawrence of taking. According to their story, Paul struck Lawrence first and the younger brother retaliated with a blow which brought blood. Paul after that slept with a club in his bed for protection." The two were so ashamed of having struck each other, neither would tell the tale.

The story was corroborated by brothers John and Lewis Sobiski, who had gone to the Keene shanty soon after. The Sobiski brothers were afraid to go to the county jail and tell the story because of the strong feelings aroused by the murders.

"Hospital attendants today stated Paul Keene would recover. Both men are in better physical condition than previously as a result of a week in jail with wholesome food and baths, and without 'hooch.'"

At 4:14 a.m. on Thursday, August 20, 1931, Fred Smith, Frank Oliver and David Blackstone were removed from the prison at Jackson and transferred to the Michigan State Prison at Marquette. The Michigan State Police transferred the three in three cars. They arrived at Marquette at 5:55 p.m. Blackstone was the first to be registered and became No. 5381, Oliver was registered next and became No. 5382 and Smith became No. 5383. The three spent the next thirty days in quarantine and then were assigned to work within the walls of the prison.

That same morning, Kate Keller was brought before Justice Jay H. Payne at the county jail for examination on the charge of being an accessory after the fact and concealing facts relative to the case. The maximum penalty for the offense was five years in a penitentiary. Keller did not know what she was to be charged with until the information was read to her. After the information had been read to her, she read the information herself. Then she was asked if she pleaded guilty or not guilty.

"I know I wouldn't plead guilty—not guilty, of course," she answered.

The date for the hearing was set for September 2, and she was held on $10,000 bond. She was then returned to her cell.

A few moments after Keller had been removed, Howard Forwalder, whose room at the Hawkins House Hotel had been searched by Harry Bennett, was brought into the court. He had been taken into custody soon after the search and had been held for questioning. Forwalder waived examination on the charge of violation of the liquor law and was immediately taken before Judge Sample. There he pleaded guilty and was remanded for sentence.

Then Otis Oden pleaded guilty to violating his parole and was sentenced by Judge Sample to one year and eleven months to two years at Jackson Prison. Oden, said Judge Sample, had no responsibility and was human in form only. It was impossible, said Judge Sample, to appeal to his mind.

On the orders of Prosecutor Rapp, Justice Payne discharged Lawrence Keene at noon. His brother Paul remained in custody, awaiting a hearing on a liquor charge.

That same day, Prosecutor Albert Rapp announced he had resigned as executor of the estate of the late Darwin Z. Curtiss, uncle of Kate Keller. She was one of the heirs to the estate. Rapp said he was withdrawing as her attorney, so he could devote full time to the case.

Daniel Vasher, who was then twenty-three years old and a friend of Frank Oliver, jointly owned the car Oliver drove on the night of the murders. Vasher was undergoing questioning by deputies on the morning of Saturday, August 29, without an attorney present. Sometime between the hours of 1:00 and 2:00 a.m., Vasher admitted an attack on a fifteen-year-old girl and an attempted attack on her thirteen-year-old sister. This attack occurred on the night of August 7. The maximum sentence for the offense was life imprisonment. Vasher further admitted to being a member of a gang with Smith and Oliver, with whom he had carried out several petting party robberies.

Vasher said he and Harvey Hubbard had attended a dance with Oliver near Willis on the night of August 8. Vasher said he had been with Smith at the Grant Street house of Kate Keller on the afternoon of August 10, the day of the murders. He said he left early in the evening.

Hubbard, according to Vasher, had made a blackjack, and he claimed Smith said it "wasn't any good and I know where we can get guns."

Vasher was then arraigned before Justice Payne; he waived examination. He was then immediately taken before Judge George Sample, where he entered a plea of guilty. He was then remanded for sentence.

That afternoon, Harvey Hubbard was charged with possession of a blackjack. He was arraigned before Justice Payne and waived examination and was bound over the circuit court. He was held in the county jail, as he was unable to furnish the $5,000 bond.

On the morning of Monday, August 31, Ted Clark was brought before Justice Payne on a charge of cohabitation with Ellen Manor, reputed to be the sweetheart of Frank Oliver. That same morning, the two were brought before Judge Sample, where they pleaded guilty and were remanded to the county jail for sentence.

Vasher and Clark were sentenced by Judge Sample on the morning of Wednesday, September 2. Vasher received a sentence of five to ten years at the state prison at Jackson, with the minimum term recommended. Clark was sentenced to six months to one year at Ionia, with the maximum term recommended.

Kate Keller was to have been arraigned that afternoon at two o'clock, but the proceeding was postponed for one week.

6
KATE KELLER

Grand Jury Ordered

On Saturday, September 5, 1931, Washtenaw County Circuit Court Judge George W. Sample announced he had ordered a one-man grand jury to investigate the role of Kate Keller in the murders of Harry Lore, Thomas Wheatley, Vivian Gold and Anna Mae Harrison. He further announced he would sit as the jury of one. The formal request was made by Deputy Lynn Squires and approved by Prosecutor Rapp. Judge Sample gave several reasons for his decision to call a grand jury:

> *Miss Keller was seen engaged in an earnest conversation with Smith the morning following the crime. She admits being with the slayers the night before the crime, at least until 9 o'clock. Clothes belonging to Smith were found in her home, the garments stained with blood. Smith was seen sleeping on a divan in the girl's home the morning following the crime. Smith was seen going toward his home the morning following the crime dressed as though he had just changed his clothing. Smith, Oliver and Blackstone, it has been learned, were with the Keller girl at a house of questionable character far into the night following the crime.*

"These facts," explained Judge Sample, "have led the court and investigating officers to believe she might even have been a principle [*sic*] in the crime."

There were three possible outcomes of the investigation: Keller could be found to have been a principal in the crimes and charged with murder, she could be indicted as an accessory after the fact (the charge under which she was then being held in the county jail) or Keller could be released if the investigation found no cause for her being held.

Judge Sample said he called the grand jury, in part, because of the good it might do the youth of the county, as the investigation might turn up information that would make it possible for officers to close "dives" and "pigs" that might be operating. For several months officers had been receiving reports of crimes, both petty and serious, being committed in the southeastern corner of the county, near the Wayne County line.

"A grand jury," noted Sample, "called for a specific purpose can always enlarge its scope and need not conclude until all necessary investigation has been made. It is not limited, and as to how far the investigation may go is problematical. I believe we may ultimately throw light on many crimes which have been committed in this county."

A grand jury is not a trial but an investigation, so the hearings are not open to the public and those present are sworn to secrecy. For this reason, those called to testify might be more likely to tell what they know before a grand jury rather than open court.

That same day, the sheriff's office issued subpoenas to twenty-three persons to appear as witnesses before the grand jury. The first grand jury hearing was set to be held on Saturday, September 12. The regular business of the court continued.

On the morning of Friday, September 11, Judge Sample denied a motion of Daniel Vasher to withdraw his plea of guilty on the statutory charge, for which he was sentenced to five to ten years in prison. By this time, Vasher had engaged an attorney, who told the court the confession made by Vasher had been made under duress and compulsion. The attorney further noted the two minor girls who had named Vasher as their attacker had changed their stories and now said Vasher did not harm them. The girls, the attorney said, were obliged to say "yes" to questions, because, the attorney said, a man named "Bill" slapped their arms.

Deputy Lynn Squires said he was present during questioning and denied any force was used.

The first session of the grand jury was held as scheduled, Saturday, September 12, and it was short. The names of the witnesses were called and told to appear on the morning of Thursday, September 17, when Edward A. Bilitzke, the Michigan assistant attorney general, was to be present to represent that office. That session was postponed, as he was unable to appear that day. The hearing was then scheduled for September 28 at 9:00 a.m.

Keller Examination

Kate Keller entered the courtroom of Justice Jay H. Payne on the afternoon of Wednesday, September 23, for examination on the charge of being an accessory after the fact, in aiding Fred Smith in an attempt to avoid justice in the Torch Murders. For her court appearance, she dressed in a plain gray dress and appeared unperturbed by the charges. Keller seated herself between her two attorneys, Kenneth Huggett and W.D. Grommon, and was, it was noted, unusually quiet.

The first witness called was Louis Osbon, who ran a gas station at 10 North Adams Street in Ypsilanti. Osbon said Fred Smith came into his station between ten and eleven o'clock on the morning after the murders, Wednesday, to use the telephone at the station. He made two calls. The first failed to go through, and Smith told Osbon he was trying call Frank Oliver. Smith told Osbon that he and Oliver intended to go into the country.

Smith made a second call, this time reaching the person he wished to speak to. Osbon told the court he heard snatches of the conversation: "What did she say?" "Yes." "Well, now, if you are going to tell her all I might as well save time and tell her in the first place."

Osbon said he later learned the second number Smith had called was the home of John Wiggett, where Kate Keller was employed.

Osbon further said he became suspicious of Smith because when they talked of the murders, Smith, instead of asking what should be done with the guilty persons, asked Osbon, "What do you suppose will be done with them?" Smith, Osbon noted, did not appear nervous.

Next witness was Gladys Wiggett of 407 Campbell Avenue, who had employed Keller since April. Keller did most of the housework and cared for Mrs. Wiggett as needed. Fred Smith, said Mrs. Wiggett, had been in the habit of calling at the house almost every night since June but had not made a practice of coming into the house.

On the night of Monday, August 10, Keller had left the house with Smith at about 6:30 and returned at about 9:30. Keller left the house about an hour later with a Mr. Duffy.

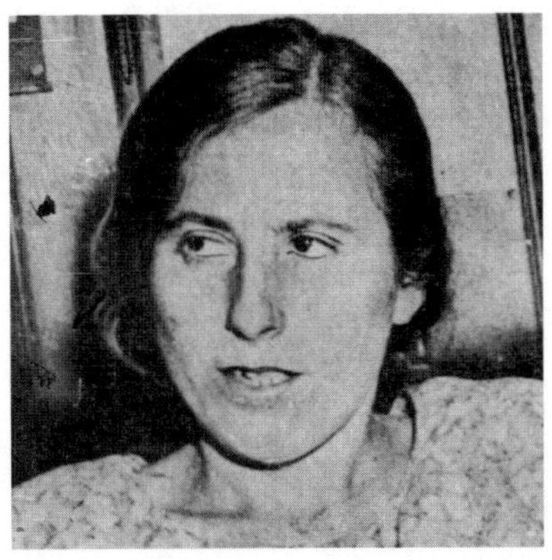

Kate Keller, the so-called sweetheart of Fred Smith, was questioned as to her part in the events of the night of August 10, 1931. She was later charged as an accomplice after the fact and convicted. *Used with permission of Tribune Content Agency.*

On Tuesday night, Smith came by the house. He did not come inside but drove up to the front of the house. Mrs. Wiggett did not know if he was alone. Keller left with Smith at about 7:00 p.m. and returned at about 9:00 pm. She left the house again at either 10:30 or 10:45 p.m., again with a Mr. Duffy. She returned home at either 12:30 or 1:00 a.m.

Keller received two telephone calls on Wednesday morning; the first was from Luella Smith, the mother of Fred Smith. Wiggett heard Keller say, "I'd rather he'd be there than living with niggers." After the call, Keller told Wiggett she had been "bawled out" by Mrs. Smith for letting Fred stay at her house at 920 Grant Street. The second call was from Fred Smith, who stopped by the house soon after and talked with her on the porch.

Under questioning from Rapp, Mrs. Wiggett said Keller had brought a gun from the Grant Street house to the Wiggett home, after the murders.

Keller spent nights at the Wiggett house and not at the house on Grant Street.

Luella Smith, the blind mother of Fred Smith, was led into the courtroom by a younger son. She gave her testimony in a clear and unwavering voice. She said she would know any person after hearing their voice twice. She said she called Keller on Wednesday morning to tell Keller she objected to her letting Fred stay at the Grant Street house.

Mrs. Smith said she received a telephone call from Keller on Thursday morning, after Fred had been taken into custody. According to Mrs. Smith, Keller said, "Fred is going to say he was home then." Keller did not ask Mrs. Smith to say Fred was home at the time of the murders.

In response, Mrs. Smith said she told Keller Fred was not at home, and she would not say Fred was home when he was not there. When asked by Grommon, attorney for Keller, if she was bitter toward the young woman, Mrs. Smith replied: "Certainly!"

Otis Odem, who was being held in the county jail as he waited to be sent to the prison at Jackson, said Smith, Blackstone and Keller had been at his place, where they had a drink together. They were there, he said, between the 6:30 and 7:00 p.m. He said they were there for about thirty minutes.

Howard Forwalder, who was awaiting sentence on violation of the prohibition law, said he had been at Otis Odem's place on Sunday, August 9, the night before the murders, with Smith, Blackstone and Oliver. Keller, he said, did not go in but had stayed in the car. When they left, Keller was seated in the front seat of the car with Oliver. Smith, Blackstone and he were seated in the back seat. They stopped at a gas station at the intersection of Huron and Washington Streets, where Blackstone obtained a flashlight.

From here, Forwalder said, they drove into town and stopped on a side street. Here Smith and Blackstone left the car. Keller became nervous and expressed a fear they might "do something." Oliver reassured her. Smith and Blackstone returned to the car and took Keller home.

Bert Curtis said he had an arrangement with Keller to take his meals at the Grant Street house. He said he was at the house at 8:00 a.m. on Tuesday, August 11, three hours after the bodies were found, where he found Smith sleeping on a settee. Curtis could not say if Smith was clothed, as Smith was covered by a blanket. This, Curtis said, was the first morning he had seen Smith there. He offered Smith breakfast, but Smith refused.

After two hours of testimony, Justice Payne ordered Keller bound over to circuit court for trial during the October term. Bond was set at $10,000 with two sureties demanded.

BODY OF CURTISS

Judge Sample began holding sessions of the grand jury on Monday, September 29, because, he said, the evidence presented during the hearing of the justice court might be insufficient to bring a conviction. A few days before this, Prosecutor Rapp had received a letter from Blackstone, informing him, "I've been doing some detective work since I have been up here and I have found out about another murder that has been committed. Fred Smith was in it." Blackstone added, he "had it in black and white" that Smith had committed another murder prior to the slayings of August 11. Blackstone wrote that he would talk only to Rapp.

Some may have wondered if this was a reference to Helen Filippow, a seven-year-old girl who had been in the care of D.Z. Curtiss at the time the time of his death. Under the provisions of the Curtiss will, Kate was named sole beneficiary on that condition she care for Helen until she came of age. The child seemed to disappear from school during the spring. As it turned out, the child was safe, having been adopted by a man in California.

"Had she remained in Kate Keller's care," noted the *Ypsilanti Daily Press* of Wednesday, September 30, 1931, "the entire estate could have been tied up until the child was of age, on grounds that there was no method of predicting how much of the Curtiss fortune would be needed to care for her in case she should become totally disabled or injured in an accident."

Luella Smith was the chief witness on Tuesday. "She has been in attendance at the jury probe since its sessions started Monday morning and does not leave the courthouse during its recess, except at night. This noon she was a pathetic figure, waiting in the lower corridor for the hearing to resume, and unwilling to leave the building for luncheon. She is accompanied by a son, younger than Fred," reported the *Ypsilanti Daily Press* of Tuesday, September 29, 1931.

At the close of the grand jury session of Tuesday, September 29, Judge Sample ordered the exhumation of the body of D.Z. Curtiss, uncle of Kate Keller, for an examination to test for traces of poison, which might have contributed to his death eight months before. Curtiss had died on February 1 after a protracted illness. The official cause of death was bronchial pneumonia and influenza and chronic prostatic enlargement. The death certificate was signed by Dr. H.B. Britton.

This decision was made after officials were told Fred Smith had told Keller he thought it best to "knock off the old judge so we can get married and live in the Grant Street house." It was said Smith had claimed to have put iodine and acid into liquor the judge drank just before passing into a coma.

He had been taken to the Ypsilanti Private Hospital a few days before he died, at his own request, friends said, as he complained of not receiving any care where he was living. Curtiss and his niece Kate Keller had given up the Grant Street house and were living temporarily in an apartment in a store on Michigan Avenue he had acquired in payment of an obligation.

"Public suspicion made it necessary to exhume Judge Curtiss' body and have the tests made," explained Judge Sample. "Judge Curtiss' open quarrel with Fred Smith provides added suspicion regarding his death."

The body of Curtiss was removed from the mausoleum at Highland Cemetery in Ypsilanti, on the morning of Wednesday, September 30, and taken to the pathology department at the University of Michigan. At the laboratory, the stomach and other vital organs were removed. The body, it was reported, was in good condition. There tests for some one hundred poisons would be carried out. The results would not be known for seven to fourteen days. The body of Curtiss was returned to the mausoleum Wednesday night.

"I hope they hurry and finish the examination of Judge Curtiss," said Keller, as she waited to testify before the grand jury the next day, the first of October. "They won't find anything. If he had lived another six weeks, he would have changed his will and put the estate in trust and there wouldn't have been all this trouble."

To this she added, "Fred isn't guilty of any other murder."

Keller had waved her right against self-incrimination and agreed to testify before the grand jury. Her testimony came after some thirty witnesses had taken the stand ahead of her.

Keller began her appearance before the grand jury on Thursday, October 1, and continued her testimony on Friday, October 2. The proceedings of the grand jury are secret and have never been made public. Once her testimony was completed, the grand jury adjourned so Rapp and Assistant Attorney General Edward Bilitzke could travel to the prison at Marquette and question Blackstone.

The two arrived at the prison on Saturday and questioned Blackstone until midnight. Rapp and Bilitzke returned to the prison on Sunday, when they questioned Smith and Oliver. Once they had finished the interviews, the two returned to Ann Arbor.

On their return to Ann Arbor, the two refused to disclose what they had learned, if anything, and remained silent on the subject. "There has been too much publicity given our work already," said Bilitzke. "We have no statement to make and will not answer no questions."

Two new witnesses were called to appear before the grand jury on Tuesday afternoon: Florence Wilson, the nurse who had attended Judge Curtiss during his last illness, and Ruth Anderson Davis, an acquaintance of Blackstone.

On that afternoon, Tuesday, October 6, 1931, Keller's arraignment was held on the charge of being an accessory after the fact before Judge Sample. Keller stood mute as the information was read. Judge Sample directed the county clerk, Claramon L. Pray, to enter a plea of "not guilty" for her. Assistant Prosecutor Carl Lehman announced the prosecution would be ready for the case to go to trial on Thursday, October 8, 1931, in two days, at 10:00 a.m.

Defense attorney Grommon protested the change, as this placed the case at the start of the October term and not at the end. This was the first defense had learned of the date of the trial. Grommon alleged that newspaper reports of the grand jury proceedings were detrimental to Keller's interests. He pointed out a newspaper story listing six reasons given by Judge Sample for calling the grand jury. This, noted Grommon, made it difficult to give Keller a fair trial.

"If I am a reasonable human being, I must have had reasons for holding the grand jury," responded Judge Sample. He added, it had been his hope, almost his wish, that Keller would be able to prove her innocence.

"I have no criticism to offer on the fairness of newspaper accounts and know of no single fact which was published but that was based on belief of truth," said Judge Sample.

"Mr. Grommon reiterated his intention of seeking a change of venue at that time and stated that affidavits which had already been prepared would be placed in the mails immediately," reported the *Ypsilanti Daily Press* of Tuesday, October 6, 1931.

That same day, Sheriff Andres received a letter from a man who identified himself as William Smith and claimed he was an eyewitness to the murders. Smith wrote that he was a nineteen-year-old hobo who had been asleep in a haystack when he was awakened by screams and pistol shots. He wrote that he saw the whole affair. "The girls were praying to God for help."

"I got a good look at all of it. I saw the pictures in the Detroit papers later and they were the rite [*sic*] ones." Smith noted that he had witnessed murders in Kansas City, Missouri and Chicago, and each time, he wrote, he was held as a suspect.

Sheriff Andres said he believed the account to be true.

KELLER ON TRIAL

The court opened at 9:00 a.m. on Thursday, October 8, 1931, and the case of Kate Keller was called. The court was packed with over 200 spectators seated, with some 50 more standing just outside the courtroom door. The total number present, including court officials, members of the bar, witnesses, reporters and those granted seats, came to about 250 people. As the roll of jurors was called, four names were removed from the list, one because he had died the previous week.

Immediately after the roll was completed, Grommon, attorney for Keller, entered a motion for a change of venue. Grommon explained, "Because of newspaper stories and because Judge Sample himself has been conducting a one-man grand jury investigating the defendant's connection with the Ypsilanti murders, we believe she cannot obtain a fair and impartial trial in this court."

To support his motion, Grommon read articles from Ann Arbor newspapers, which he said were prejudiced against Keller. Grommon said he did not question Judge Sample's fairness in conducting the trial.

Assistant Washtenaw County Prosecutor Carl Lehman said he wished for Keller to receive a fair trial and added that since Wednesday morning, fifty-five affidavits had been submitted opposing a change in venue. "The affidavits," noted the *Ypsilanti Daily Press* of Thursday, October 8, 1931, "were signed by bankers, jewelers, merchants, professional and tradesmen." Keller was pale and appeared nervous during the plea for a change of venue. She spent part of the time perusing a letter.

Lehman, regarding the change in venue motion, cited a case in which Judge Sample denied such a motion, a decision that was upheld by the Michigan State Supreme Court.

Judge Sample denied the motion for a change of venue, saying it would be difficult to find a county in Michigan where the murders had not been covered in the local press. The case, in fact, had been the subject of national interest. Judge Sample expressed his wish for Keller to prove her innocence. He added if in impaneling a jury that it proved impossible to form one that was impartial, he would reconsider the motion for a change in venue.

After the motion for a change of venue had been denied, the process of choosing a jury began. Under questioning, one prospective juror, Elmer Gage, a farmer from Sharon Township, said he lived within ten miles of where the murders had been committed and said he knew nothing of the crime. "Reporters," noted the *Michigan Daily* of October 9, 1931, "thought their papers had informed everyone in the state about the killings."

Keller appeared calm during the selection of the jury, sitting back in her chair with her chin in her hand. She also munched on a box of candy, the present of a reporter. During the morning proceedings, Keller wore a light-yellow dress, and during the noon recess she changed to a gray suit for the afternoon.

The jury was selected by early afternoon and consisted of eleven men: nine farmers, one businessman and a contractor. There was one woman on the jury, a housewife.

Once the jury was selected, the court adjourned to reconvene the next morning.

Court opened promptly the next morning at nine and began with Prosecutor Rapp stating the case against Kate Keller. As part of his opening statement, Rapp detailed the events of the night of August 10, the murders of Lore, Wheatley, Gold and Harrison. Defense attorney Grommon objected to the recounting of the murders on the grounds it would influence the jury. Judge Sample overruled the objection, as it was necessary to prove a crime had been committed.

"Points which the state expects to prove," summarized the *Ypsilanti Daily Press* of Friday, October 9, 1931, "are that Miss Keller was at the Odem blind pig with Smith the night preceding the crimes, was with him when a flashlight was obtained at a gasoline station at the intersection of Washington and Huron Sts.: that she was fearful on that occasion that 'something might happen'; that Smith was on the divan of her home at 9 o'clock the morning following the crime; that she harbored him and gave him money; that on the same day she washed clothes at the Anna Titus home and on the way back to her Campbell Ave. address stopped to buy a paper containing news of the crimes; that she was with Smith that night with two other parties at the Grant St. home; that two days after the slayings she told officers clothing in her Grant St. house was that worn by Smith the night of the crimes; and that when she was released, after her first arrest, she made the remark that the best thing she could do was to leave town till 'this thing blows over.'"

Objections were raised over Rapp describing the conduct of Keller and Smith at the Grant Street house as "lewd and lascivious." Rapp asserted it was necessary to prove Keller and Smith were on "friendly terms." Judge Sample overruled the objection.

Louis Osbon was among the first witnesses called, and he recounted hearing what Smith said on the phone the day after the bodies were found.

John Wiggett, who employed Keller at his house at 407 Campbell Avenue, told the court Keller was accustomed to visiting her house on Grant Street nearly every night and often did so in the company of Fred Smith. Keller, he explained, was expected to spend nights at the Campbell Avenue house. About two weeks before the murders, Wiggett found Keller returning to the Wiggett house at 6:30 a.m. He said Keller had been out with Smith the night before.

On the Sunday night before the murders, Wiggett said, Keller had left the house with Smith and Oliver. He did not know when she had returned. On the Monday night of the murders, Wiggett said, Smith and Oliver stopped by the house for Keller. That night, and the two nights after, Keller left the house at 10:30 p.m. and went out with a Mr. Duffy, a cookie salesman.

On the night of the murders, Wiggett said, Smith wore a blue shirt.

Keller, according to Wiggett, explained her almost nightly visits to the Grant Street house, to feed her cat and pick up her mail.

Otis Odem said Keller had been at his blind pig one or two times before the night of the murders and had been served liquor. He did not know for sure if Blackstone drank with her. Odem was not sure if Keller and the others—Smith, Oliver and Blackstone—joined the dancing at his blind pig. He said it was not unusual for white persons to frequent his place of business. The jury heard him tell of Blackstone giving him the gun the morning after the murders.

Now former Deputy Sheriff Lynn Squires took the stand. Squires had been dismissed from the Washtenaw County Sheriff's Department by Sheriff Andres for reasons that were never publicly explained. The most likely reason was Squires may have conducted aspects of the investigation without the knowledge and approval of Sheriff Andres. On the stand, Squires told the court that a light purple striped shirt and gray striped trousers, which were offered into evidence, had been turned over to him by Keller as the clothing Smith wore on the night of the murders. John Wiggett had testified Smith was dressed in a blue shirt on the night of the murders.

Smith had been arrested at 8:30 a.m. and made his confession at 4:30 p.m. Squires said he went to the Campbell house and from there went with Keller to the house on Grant Street. There, Squires said, Keller turned over to him the lavender striped shirt.

Squires told of questioning Keller in March regarding Smith as part of an investigation into petty thievery. He said he asked her if she had seen Smith carry a gun or if she knew if he was in possession of stolen property. Keller told Squires she had loaned Smith a gun, a nickel-plated revolver, that had belonged to her uncle. This, she said, was for use during rabbit season. Keller told Squires that Smith had returned the gun, and she had placed it where he could not find it. She said it had not been stolen.

Howard Forwalder, who was awaiting sentencing on violation of the prohibition law, said he made his home at the Hawkins House Hotel and had been living there since the week before the Fourth of July. He had been employed as a laborer at the Ypsilanti State Hospital, then under construction. He said he first met Keller about two weeks before the murders at Lowell Beach, a dance hall.

On the Saturday before the murders, Forwalder said, Smith, Keller and he went to the Lowell Beach dance hall. He and Smith had placed moonshine liquor in the car in which they rode, with Keller, to the hall. The liquor had been taken to the Grant Street house that day in a jug, and he and Smith had bottled it there. Defense attorney Grommon tried to show Keller did not know about the liquor but was not successful. The next night, Sunday, Forwalder delivered liquor to the blind pig run by Odem.

On the Monday of the week before the murders, Smith and Forwalder went to the Wiggett house between 6:30 and 7:00 p.m., where they picked up Keller. From there they went to the house on Grant Street, where they were joined by Oliver. The three then went to the Odem blind pig, where they were joined by Blackstone. They stayed only a short time, and left between 7:00 and 7:30 p.m.

They stopped at the gas station at the intersection of Huron and Washington Streets. Smith and Blackstone got out of the car, while Oliver, Forwalder and Keller remained behind. Keller, Forwalder said, expressed a fear the two were planning a holdup, and said "she knew they would do something" if they brought Blackstone along. Forwalder said Keller started to get out of the car but resumed her seat when Smith and Blackstone came back into view.

On the evening after the murders, Tuesday, Forwalder said he went to the Grant Street house, where he got Smith, and they went to the Wiggett house, where they were joined by Keller, and then returned to the house on Grant Street. Forwalder left the two there for almost an hour. The prosecution made Forwalder recount the movements of the two. This was to show they had time for a conference.

At the end of Forwalder's testimony, the court adjourned until Monday.

Helen Twist testified she was at the Grant Street house on the evening of Tuesday, August 11, the day the bodies were found, and saw Keller and Smith holding a conversation in the kitchen. The two, she said, were alone. She said she did not hear what they were talking about. Keller left the kitchen and went to join the others in the living room, where stories were told that, Twist said, "she was unwilling to repeat in the court room."

Glen Hart, a student at the Michigan State Normal College, now Eastern Michigan University, took the stand to talk about the ride he had with Keller on the night of the trial of Smith, Oliver and Blackstone. Keller had been taken to the Washtenaw County Jail that evening and, after questioning, was returned home, driven by Hart and Richard Skinner, also a student at the Normal College. According to Hart, Keller said, "No one can make me believe he did it." She said he had been "scared into confessing," and officers "always had it in for him."

She told Hart and Skinner she had been aroused by a deputy sheriff who had questioned her. She spoke of the deputy in what Hart said was "extremely profane" language. "If he doesn't leave me alone," she added, "I'll bust him with a beer bottle. I think I'd better leave town until this blows over."

Madden Duty was called to testify about when, two months before the murders, he had spent the night at the Grant Street house. In the night, Eunice Keller, sister of Kate, had come to his bed, where they had sexual intercourse. As a result, Eunice became pregnant. Under cross-examination, Duty was asked about his reluctance to give testimony before the grand jury.

Luella Smith, Fred's mother, took the stand on the morning of Tuesday, October 13, 1931, and said Kate called her on the Thursday after the murders and asked her to lie and say Fred was home at the time of the murders. "I refused," she said, "because I wouldn't lie even to save Fred from jail."

She told of burning pictures of Keller, Fred and his younger brother Sam because they were "too filthy to have around the house."

"Other testimony given by Mrs. Smith was relative to Miss Keller's gun which she stated had been in Fred's possession at the farm. It was given to Miss Keller at the farm home, and she promised not to let Fred have it again, the witness stated. Mrs. Smith herself took the weapon to Candyland (a candy store in Ann Arbor) at a later date and again requested Miss Keller not to let Fred have it, she testified," reported the *Ypsilanti Daily Press* of Tuesday, October 13, 1931.

Mrs. Smith said she had been blind since she was a child but could tell colors. She said Fred had been at the farm Saturday morning before the murders and had taken a blue shirt from the clothes basket.

She was asked why Fred left home on the Thursday previous to the murders. "He had no reason to leave," she replied, "only just to go down and live with her again. We never could figure out why he left."

Mrs. Smith denied there had been trouble at home over the use of the car. "How could he?" she answered. "He had it seven days and seven nights a week."

Under cross-examination, Grommon asked Mrs. Smith about a visit to the farm on the Wednesday after the murders by Clinton LeForge, Ypsilanti attorney, and Wayne County Sheriff Deputies George Frahm and Lewis Chamberlain. The men had come to the farm to question Fred. Grommon asked her if Fred had asked her, "Ma, where was I Monday night?" To this question, Grommon asked if she had said, "I don't know, that's the night it rained." She denied giving as her answer, "Monday night? That's the night it rained, why, you were home." Mrs. Smith denied she heard Fred say he was home Monday night when questioned by the officers.

In response to a question by Grommon regarding Keller, Mrs. Smith answered, "I feel she is the root of evil in these crimes. If my son had been at home instead of at her house, he would not have been involved in the murders."

Samuel Smith, the sixteen-year-old brother of Fred, testified he knew Keller owned a revolver and had used the weapon for target practice during the summer of 1930. He said he had not seen the gun since that time.

Bert Curtis, who had meals at the Grant Street house, said he arrived at the house at about 8:00 a.m. on Tuesday and found Smith on the divan. He said Smith's face looked unusually dark. Smith was covered with a blanket, but one shoulder was visible, so Curtis saw Smith was not wearing a shirt. Curtis said he offered Smith some breakfast, but Smith replied, "No I guess I won't get up."

Curtis said that as he was eating breakfast, he noticed a pair of oxfords under the china closet, and they appeared to have been recently cleaned. Curtis said the peculiar behavior of Smith and the condition of the shoes caused him to become suspicious. He said he told Chief of Police Ralph Southard about his suspicions on Wednesday, but no action was taken at that time.

Curtis was followed on the stand by Hallie Hart, who also had meals at the Grant Street house and was there at the same time as Curtis. She said she saw Smith there, and one side of his face looked "singed" and he had a "wild and desperate" appearance. "I never saw a human being look like that before," she said. When Curtis made a comment about the water-soaked oxfords, she made a motion for him to keep quiet. Later, Mrs. Hart said, she advised Keller against letting Smith stay at the house.

The jury was dismissed from the courtroom while Wayne County Deputies Lewis Chamberlain and George Frahm gave testimony. The two had been to the Smith farm the day before his arrest and asked his mother where he had been on Monday night. According to them, she had said, "It was raining that night, you were home." On the stand, Mrs. Smith denied the statement. She had told the court she would not tell a lie, not even to save her son from prison. Judge Sample ruled the testimony of the deputies inadmissible, as it would impeach the testimony of Mrs. Smith. This left Keller as the only defense witness.

Gladys Wiggett was to have testified for the defense but was too ill to attend the trial. She did give a deposition, in which she said the shirt Keller had washed at the Titus home on Tuesday morning, the one Fred Smith was said to have worn during the murders, had "no blood stains on it." The deposition was read to the jury.

All eyes in the crowded courtroom were on Kate Keller as she rose from her seat to take the stand in her own defense. Under questioning by her attorney, Grommon, she began with a recitation of her life. She had lived in Missouri until she was nineteen and had left school in the tenth grade because of illness. She came to Ypsilanti to care for her aunt who was ill and, after her passing, stayed with her uncle as housekeeper. Over the next six years, the two were involved in a number of charitable projects. "There was always someone there," she said.

When asked "Who?" she explained there was one man who had no place to live, wandered into the house and stayed a year. Her brother had stayed at the house, as had Fred Smith, who was there when her uncle was still alive. There was the little girl who had run away from her family and was given shelter at the house for a time. A whole family with five children were taken in for a time. Two of the children were still at the house when her uncle died. She had cared for her uncle in his last illness, and this, she said, was the reason why she was the beneficiary of his estate.

She first met Fred Smith in March 1930.

"I met Fred in Ionia Reformatory, where I had driven his mother, Mrs. Louella [*sic*] Smith, at her request. I liked him very much that year, but not so much this year. My uncle had helped Fred get a parole and had approved of our friendship before his death."

When asked by Grommon why she continued to go out with Smith when she no longer cared that much for him, she answered, "Just somewhere to go nights, I guess."

"But I had no intention of marrying Fred. He was a friend and I helped him by letting him live at my house."

Fred, she said, had told her of his difficulties at home and that he had been forced to leave. "The first night he was away from home he slept under a tree on 'nigger' hill," she said. Keller offered to let him stay at the Grant Street house. Keller said she called the Smith farm to let the family know where he was. She talked to his father, who, she said, told her, "When you see him tell him to come and get his clothes, he's through here."

When asked about the night she rode in a car with Oliver, Smith, Blackstone and Howard Forwalder, she denied she had been worried Smith and Blackstone were going to hold up someone. "I was angry because Blackstone was in the car with me," declared Keller, "but I didn't say anything about a holdup." According to her story, she said, "What if the police should see me with that funny looking nigger in the car."

"I don't dance," said Keller. "I went to Lowell Beach with Fred and Forwalder the Saturday before the murders to see the place. When I learned Forwalder had liquor in the car and was trying to sell it, I started crying and offered him $1 to drive me home. We had come in Forwalder's car."

"Monday night, the night of the crime, about 8:30 o'clock, I noticed Fred's blue shirt was dirty. I told him to give it to me and I would wash it the following day, which I did with Mrs. Gladys Wiggett, for whom I worked. I left Fred about 9 o'clock that night and the murders weren't until much later. I got Fred a shirt of my uncle's, which the prosecutors have introduced here, and he put that on. The last time I saw Fred was in Jackson prison after he had been sentenced. I told him I would write. He kissed me goodbye."

Cross-examination was carried out by State Assistant Attorney General Edward Bilitzke, who questioned Keller on a number of subjects, including two diamond settings that had gone missing from the Grant Street house and visits to fortune tellers in Toledo and Detroit. These visits were with Fred Smith and his mother. One such visit had occurred on Election Day in November 1930; Keller said, "I hurried home to vote for Mr. Rapp."

Under questioning, she at first denied her uncle objected to her going out with Smith but admitted the previous winter he had told her Smith "was not good enough for you."

Bilitzke questioned Keller on a letter she had received purporting to be from her sister Eunice. In the letter, Eunice asked Kate for suggestions of how to relieve herself of a pregnancy.

"She said emphatically," reported the *Ypsilanti Daily Press* of Thursday, October 15, 1931, "that she never remembered the contents of letters and refused to give testimony on parts suggested to her by the state's lawyers."

"Cross questioning on her story with the regard to the shirt worn by Smith the night of the slayings failed to change her former statement even thought it was recalled to her mind that Smith, when she visited him in Jackson prison, stated that he had removed the shirt on the way back to Ypsilanti Tuesday morning following the slayings and had torn it up, throwing it out of the car," noted the account.

Under questioning, Keller revealed that Fred Smith had proposed marriage to her two days after the murders. Smith told Keller the people occupying the tenant house at his father's farm were moving out soon, and he suggested she marry him so they could live in that house.

"I didn't want to live on no farm," said Keller before the jury, which included nine farmers.

The prosecution called only one rebuttal witness, Ruth Anderson Davis, an African American woman, who testified on the afternoon of Wednesday, October 14, 1931, saying that on the Monday night before the murders, she, Keller, Fred Smith, and David Blackstone left the Oden blind pig and went to the Grant Street house. There, according to Mrs. Davis, Keller invited all of them into the house.

All of them, according to Mrs. Davis, went into the house. Keller, she said, took them through the house, being careful not to turn on the lights on the first floor. They were at the house at about midnight and left after twenty or thirty minutes. Mrs. Davis said she was driven home by Smith, with Blackstone in the same car.

"Miss Keller," reported the *Ypsilanti Daily Press* of Thursday, October 15, 1931, "through her testimony Wednesday afternoon and this morning all but screamed denials that Blackstone had been in her house at that time."

When Bilitzke questioned her about the visit, she shouted, in an almost hysterical tone, "Blackstone was never in my house." She added, "Don't you say that to me again."

Keller said she feared Blackstone because "his hair stood up and his eyes bulged out."

After completion of her testimony, the trial entered its final stage, with the attorneys making their concluding arguments before the jury. The prosecution painted an image of Keller as a fallen woman, while the defense tried to paint her as a fallen angel.

"Seeing Fred Smith in blind pigs, knowing he had been out of work for months, knowing his prison record, meeting him in prison, and knowing his character as a man, the defendant must have suspected him of complicity in these crimes," said Bilitzke in his concluding statement. He reviewed the testimony, the telephone conversation overheard by Osbon, the effort to have Mrs. Smith say Fred was home that Monday night, the shirt she turned over while saying it was the one Fred wore that night.

Even the good-bye kiss Smith gave her at Jackson Prison was made note of. "She," said Bilitzke, "knowing that his hands were dripping with the blood of those innocent children, allowed him to press his lips to hers."

The defense called this a "kiss of pity."

"We want justice in this case," said Grommon, "not vengeance: we hope that the cries of the mob have faded out. We want only a decision which will satisfy your consciences."

"The Curtiss home was a haven of refuge for those who were down and out. She lived in an environment of people who wanted to help somebody," noted Grommon. He reminded the jury that Keller came to live with her uncle at the age of nineteen, to care for her relation, and stayed to care for her uncle. "She was young, Judge Curtiss was the same as a father to her. Whatever he sanctioned, what seemed right to him was right to her. When Judge Curtiss realized that Smith's companionship was not desirable for his niece, her friendship had already ripened into love and the emotion was not easily cast aside," noted Grommon. He added that Justice Curtiss had taken Smith into his home "to give him a boost instead of a knock."

At the conclusion of his remarks, Grommon pointed to the wall behind the jury box, where the "Oath of allegiance" was displayed with the phrase "with liberty and justice for all."

The closing argument for the prosecution was made by Carl Lehman, who asserted Keller had tried to assist Smith by turning over a shirt to Deputy Lynn Squires she said was the one worn by Smith. "From midnight to 5 o'clock the morning of August 11 Blackstone and Smith were lugging those children, shot and defiled. Blackstone's shirt was so bloody that he threw it in the fire, but Katherine Keller produces one for Lynn Squires with-out a speck of blood on it, one that she said Smith wore while he was beating the life out of Harry Lore with a stone. That fact alone is sufficient to point the finger of condemnation at the respondent in this case."

The next morning, Friday, October 16, 1931, Judge Sample charged the jury, telling them to weigh the circumstantial evidence. To find Keller guilty, she must have known of the crime and, with this knowledge, gave assistance to Fred Smith. It did not matter if the assistance was effectual. Should the jury find she had this knowledge and did give assistance to Smith, then the jury must find her guilty. Sample reminded the jury they should have listened to the case with the presumption that Keller was innocent. The case was given to the jury at 10:40 a.m.

The jury retired, and on the first ballot the vote was ten for conviction, one for acquittal and one blank. On the second ballot, the vote was ten for conviction and two for acquittal. The third ballot was eleven for conviction and one for acquittal. The fourth ballot was unanimous for conviction.

The jury returned to the courtroom at 11:52 a.m., one hour and fourteen minutes after receiving their charge, to announce their verdict of guilty. The jury made a recommendation for leniency.

Judge Sample was to impose a sentence on Saturday, at 9:00 a.m., but this was to be delayed until the court received the report on the autopsy on the body of Justice Curtiss.

"I could not find presence of any poison that would account for or be a factor in the death of D.Z. Curtiss," said Dr. Herbert W. Emerson, toxicologist at the University of Michigan, when he submitted his report on the autopsy on Thursday, October 22, 1931. Death, it was determined, was due to pneumonia, as stated on the death certificate. Smith had said he had put iodine and acid into the liquor Curtiss drank just before passing into a coma, not long before he died.

"If Smith actually did attempt to poison the Judge, insufficient [amounts] of the drugs, or a counter-acting combination was used, which passed through his system leaving no trace which the toxicological examination could reveal," noted the *Ypsilanti Daily Press* of that date.

Judge Sample passed sentence of four to five years at the Detroit House of Correction on Kate Keller at 12:15 p.m. on Saturday, October 24, one week after her conviction. The courtroom was filled with one of the largest crowds since the trial began, to hear sentence passed. Judge Sample said that after hearing the testimony of the grand jury proceedings and during the trial, he was thoroughly convinced of her guilt. "Your close association with the murderers, both preceding and succeeding the crimes convinces me that you knew all about what had been done," said Judge Sample. Her two months' stay in the county jail, he said, had failed to improve her attitude.

"If," said Judge Sample, "after two and a half years, you show evidence of a change in your conduct, speech, and thoughts, I will intercede for your release at that time. Otherwise, the full term will be imposed."

When asked if she had anything to say, Keller replied, "I'd just like to be given another chance."

Keller was returned to the county jail in time for the noon meal. Then she packed her few belongings and was taken to the Detroit House of Correction at Plymouth that afternoon. She was taken there by Sheriff Andres and his wife, who had been appointed matron at the jail the week before.

"One of my friends in Ann Arbor is now planning to take my case to the Supreme Court," said Keller on her arrival at the Detroit House of Correction. Then she underwent a physical examination and changed into prison attire. In an interview with prison officials, she was asked what occupation she preferred to follow during her term. She chose nursing, as, she explained, she had cared for her uncle during his last illness.

"I expect to get out on bond for a new trial," she told Captain Edward Dennison, prison superintendent, "but I'm going to be a good prisoner while I'm here."

Keller blamed Luella Smith for her fate. "She told me," said Kate, "if Fred ever got into trouble again, she was going to make it tough for the girl he was going with, and she has."

At the Detroit House of Correction, Keller was confined to a colony consisting of eight cottages with twenty-eight women residing in each building. This colony included a hospital, a dining hall, a laundry, offices and other buildings. During her time here, she was assigned to work as a check girl in the laundry and performed other tasks as well. Each woman had her own room with hot and cold water and a bed. There was a radio and a piano in each cottage as well. The women entertained themselves with music, dances and plays they performed themselves. Keller had plenty to fill her time as she awaited the results of her appeal to the Michigan State Supreme Court.

REQUEST FOR NEW TRIAL

A motion for a new trial for Keller was filed in the office of the Washtenaw County Clerk on Wednesday, November 4, 1931, by her attorney, W.D. Grommon. The motion alleged errors and irregularities as grounds for a new trial. The alleged errors and irregularities included denial of motion for a change of venue; permitting the prosecutor to detail the circumstances of the Torch Murders, which were prejudicial to the jury; permitting testimony given by Smith and Oliver at their trial to be read in open court; overruling a motion to require Smith and Oliver to be produced in court, where they could be subject to cross-examination; refusal to allow the testimony of Wayne County Deputies Lewis Frahm and George Chamberlain; "and that there is grave doubt that Miss Keller is guilty of the charge for which she was sentenced."

Judge Sample denied the motion for a new trial, and an appeal was then made to the Michigan State Supreme Court. The State of Michigan did not have a court of appeals until after the adoption of a new state constitution in 1963. Until then, appeals were submitted to the Michigan State Supreme

Court, which acted as a court of appeals. The appeal was submitted to the court on October 13, 1932. The case was decided on January 3, 1933. The court reversed the conviction and ordered a new trial.

"The defendant has assigned error on rulings of the court permitting in evidence many acts and circumstances showing defendant's association and intimacy with Fred Smith prior to the murder," noted the court.

"It was competent for the people to show Smith's character and defendant's intimacy with him as bearing not only on her knowledge that he committed the crime but also on the probability that she would harbor him and assist in enabling him to escape conviction."

The court found error in the testimony of Madden Duty and his spending the night with Eunice Keller, the sister of Kate, two months before the murders, and the fact the two had sexual intercourse. "The testimony was wholly irrelevant and should have been excluded, but we are not inclined to hold it ground for reversal. The immorality of the defendant was so well known to the jury from other competent evidence that one more immoral act from another member of her family could not have injuriously affected her standing."

Burt Curtis had told of the shoes he saw at the Grant house the day after the murder, which appeared to have been washed, causing Curtis to become suspicious. "The testimony shows that the defendant was not present at that time and did not go to the house at all during the day but was there later in the evening. There is no testimony that she had seen the shoes or knew of their condition....Without in some way connecting the defendant with knowledge of the condition of the shoes, the testimony was incompetent and should not have been received."

The court assigned error in excluding the testimony of Wayne County Deputies Louis Chamberlain and George Fram in regard to where Fred Smith spent Monday night. His mother, Luella Smith, the deputies said, had told them he had been at home that night, "so when the defendant's counsel crossed-examined Luella Smith as to these claims and what she told the officers about them, they were interrogating her in regard to material matters. The defendant was not bound by her answers. The testimony of the officers was a fair impeachment. In excluding it the court erred."

The court concluded the testimony of Luella Smith in regard to the indecent pictures was beyond what was necessary to show a relationship between Keller and Smith.

"Considered independently, these matters may not have been sufficiently prejudicial to warrant reversal, but in combination, their effect must have been to create a courtroom atmosphere at least unfriendly to the defendant. The trial of the case followed closely an atrocious murder. The defendant's prior intimacy with those concerned in that crime placed her in an unfavorable light with the jury, and it should not have been augmented by matters which reflected on her and shed no light on the issue."

"Under difficult circumstances," the court concluded, "the record shows that the circuit judge was painstaking in his effort to give the defendant a fair and impartial trial. His charge was clear and fair, and in the main on his part the trial was well conducted. But the record also shows errors on account of which the judgment of conviction must be reversed. It is reversed, and a new trial granted."

In the end, the decision was made not to hold a second trial, and Keller was released from the Detroit House of Corrections on May 3, 1933, seventeen months after her conviction. For her, the ordeal was over.

7

ENDINGS

Her time at the Detroit House of Corrections does not seem to have improved Kate Keller's choice of companions, as she was taken into custody by Detroit police on the morning of Wednesday, June 13, 1934. She was in the company of Frank Smiley, twenty-eight, and Edward Ward, twenty-two, both of Ann Arbor. The two young men were both paroled convicts. Smiley and Ward had served time for armed robbery convictions at Jackson Prison. Detroit police found the three in a car at Livernois and Grand River Avenues. A pistol was found in the car. The car was similar to the one used in several holdups. Smiley and Ward were held for police in Ann Arbor, as the two were suspected of the attempted holdup of a grocer the previous Monday. Keller was held for investigation. She said she was employed as a domestic.

The estate of her uncle D.Z. Curtiss appears to have been still in probate, as the administrator, Clinton Le Forge, was charged with larceny by conversion in December 1935. Le Forge was charged with issuing checks that were not accounted for in the records of the estate.

"I have never received anything for my services during four years as administrator," said Le Forge. "Half of the amount I am accused of taking would go as fees. The receipts for expenditures which I have not produced are in the possession of my wife."

The prosecutor was Albert J. Rapp, who had been the administrator of the Curtiss estate until he resigned to prosecute the case against Kate Keller. Rapp was replaced as administrator by Clinton Le Forge. As a result of the case, Le Forge lost his license to practice law.

The law was not done with the Torch Murders yet.

Walter M. Nelson, as attorney for Frank Oliver, filed a new trial petition on July 18, 1949, in the Washtenaw County Circuit Court. According to the petition, Nelson contended Oliver was subject to beatings by arresting officers and forced to confess his part in the crime. Further, Oliver did not understand what was happening during the proceedings and was not accurately represented by legal counsel. The preliminary hearing, arraignment trial and sentencing were held within four hours. Oliver was influenced by the mob outside the courthouse threatening to lynch him and the others. Judge George Sample was prejudiced in his handling of the case.

The hearing on the petition was held on March 4, 1950, at the Washtenaw County Courthouse, perhaps in the same room where the trial had been held. Oliver sat impassively all through the three-hour hearing. The hearing was held before Judge James R. Breakey Jr., who had succeeded the late Judge Sample.

"His guilt or innocence is practically irrelevant in this matter," said Nelson. The question before the court, Nelson asserted, was whether proceedings were just. Oliver, said Nelson, was "so shocked and dazed that he was going around like an automaton. Here's a boy who had no training which would enable him to evaluate what was going to happen to him. Oliver was immediately subjected to assault and torture upon his arrest, was suddenly among strange and unfriendly people, and less than an hour later was told at the bar that a Mr. Mellott was his attorney. Mr. Mellott tells all three of them to plead guilty, whispering from behind. The form was gone through, but the substance was utterly lacking."

No legal court was in session, said Nelson, when Oliver and the others stood trial, and "with a mob howling outside, there is no judicial calm."

The four lifetime sentences, said Nelson, were improperly imposed, as Oliver did not know "which of the four he is spending his life for."

Judge Breakey read from part of the eighteen pages of Oliver's testimony before Judge Sample and noted he had been advised of his constitutional right not to make a statement. "His answers," said Judge Breakey, "show that he wasn't just yessing the prosecutor." Judge Breakey called the eighteen pages of testimony "a complete statement of guilt."

Oliver, noted Judge Breakey, knew what he had done.

"A man who can do what he did and see what he saw and then go out and paint a house the next day, well I needn't comment on it."

"I think," continued Judge Breakey, "he showed excellent judgment in pleading guilty. He could have had all the lawyers it was possible to marshal and looked up all the law, but on that 18 pages of testimony he was guilty of first-degree murder."

The petition for a new trial was denied.

That same year, 1950, David Blackstone died in the prison at Marquette. The official cause of death was a heart attack. There is a rumor that fellow inmates pushed him under a stone crusher.

Fred Smith died in his sleep at Marquette in February 1967. Smith was said to have had an excellent record as a prisoner.

During his time in prison, Oliver attended commercial school and became chief clerk in the school office. He was later given a position of trust in the inmate store and held the position for nineteen years. Oliver earned an instructor certificate in civil defense and was a member of the reformatory rescue team. He earned a certificate in hospital administration. Oliver, while still in prison, earned a license to operate a nursing home in Oregon.

Oliver was described by a prison newspaper in February 1966 as "a quiet little guy who plods along doing his work—not just what is expected of him, but usually more. Always he has been known for his willingness to help others."

The Michigan State Parole Board submitted a recommendation favoring the release of Oliver to the office of Michigan Governor George Rommey in November 1967. Because those convicted of first-degree murder, as Oliver was, are not eligible for parole, his sentence first had to be commuted to a lesser one before parole could be granted. This was done, and Oliver was released from prison in 1969 at the age of fifty-seven. He moved to Oregon, where he was employed as an administrator of a nursing home. In 1973, he started a program to interview suspects to aid in deciding which could be released on personal recognizance while awaiting trial. The program was successful in choosing which of those could be released and would not flee or be a risk to the community.

Near the end of his life, Oliver returned to Ypsilanti to be near his family when he died. With the passing of Frank Oliver, the story of the Torch Murders ends.

What Became of Them After

Bert Lore was an unemployed carpenter at the time of the murders. Afterward, Harry Bennett found him employment at the Ford Motor

Company. He died at the age of seventy-eight on January 17, 1960, and is buried in Highland Cemetery, near his son Harry.

Jacob Andres continued to hold the office of Washtenaw County sheriff until September 20, 1940, when he died of a heart attack while working at his desk. He was fifty-one years of age.

Albert Rapp held the office of prosecuting attorney for Washtenaw County until 1940, when he returned to private practice. He died in March 1966.

Ralph Southard stepped down as chief of police in 1943 but continued with the department as assistant chief until his retirement in 1946. He died on December 1, 1953, at the age of seventy-seven.

Harry Toy held the office of Wayne County prosecutor until 1935, when he was elected attorney general for the State of Michigan. In October 1935, Toy was appointed to the Michigan State Supreme Court to fill a vacancy. He was defeated for reelection in 1936. He served as commissioner of the Detroit Police Department from 1947 to 1950. Toy was planning to run for governor of Michigan when on September 9, 1955, at the age of sixty-three, he died of a heart attack.

As the investigation into the murders was being conducted, the government of Wayne County offered a reward of $3,000 to anyone who could provide information leading to the arrest and conviction of the killers. At the same time, the *Detroit Free Press* offered an additional reward of $1,000, and the *Detroit Times* offered a reward of $1,000 as well. The decision of who would receive the reward was made by Wayne County Prosecutor Harry Toy, who decided it would be evenly divided between Frank Johnson, who shared his suspicions of Blackstone with Ypsilanti Chief of Police Ralph Southard, and George Nelms, who turned in the murder weapon to Southard.

In the years after the Torch Murders, Harry Bennett would claim he received a tip from the police as to the identity of a suspect in the case. Bennett would say, in the early hours of the morning, he went to where the suspect was staying and took him into custody. Then, said Bennett, he conveyed the suspect to his castle overlooking the Huron River, where, he said, he tortured a confession out of him. Bennett said his actions were justified, as it saved two innocent men, the Keene brothers, from a miscarriage of justice. There is no reason to believe the story, as there is only Bennett's word that it is true. He most likely told the story to build up his image of a tough guy. Still, it is the only story about the Torch Murders anyone who knows anything about it is likely to have heard.

Bennett continued as head of the Ford Service Department until 1945, when he was fired by Henry Ford II. Bennett died at the Beverly Manor Nursing Home in Los Gatos, California, on January 4, 1979. At the time of his death, Bennett was eighty-six years of age.

No longer a detective with the Washtenaw County Sheriff Department, Lynn Squires found employment in the Ford Motor Company Service Department under Harry Bennett. Squires carried out his own private investigation of the murder of eight-year-old Richard Streicher in March 1935. Streicher was stabbed to death and his body left under the footbridge connecting Frog Island to Cross Street. The case was never solved. Squires died on June 28, 1960, at the age of seventy-one.

Edward Deake, who, at the age of ten, had watched as Smith, Blackstone and Oliver were led through the crowd in front of the Ypsilanti City Hall, followed through with his interest in law. He received his law degree from the University of Michigan in 1946. In 1950, he was elected justice of the peace for the City of Ypsilanti and municipal judge for the city in 1953. Then in 1968 Deake was elected judge in the Fourteenth District and in 1972 was elected circuit court judge for the Twenty-Second Judicial Circuit. He held the office of circuit court judge until his retirement in 1990. Judge Deake presided over the preliminary hearing of John Norman Collins, accused of the first-degree murder of Karen Sue Beineman, on August 7, 1969. Beineman was the last victim of the Co-ed Killer, also known as the Michigan Murders.

AFTERWARD

What was known as Peninsular Grove in 1931 is now a city park. Apartment houses had been constructed just north of the grove by the 1980s. Students residing in the apartments used the grove as a shortcut to the campus of Eastern Michigan University. In May 1983, the body of Laura Jean McBride, a twenty-six-year-old student at Eastern, was found hidden in a clump of bushes in the grove. She had been raped and stabbed to death.

The grove was owned by the Peninsula Paper Mill, directly across the Huron River from the Grove. Soon after the murder, the grove was sold to the city for one dollar. The city turned the grove into a city park.

The murder of Laura Jean McBride remained unsolved for the next twenty-four years, until a suspect was identified through DNA matching.

The suspect was serving a life sentence for a previous crime. He received a second life sentence for the Laura Jean McBride murder.

The Peninsula Paper Mill was closed and demolished and is now the site of Peninsula Place apartments.

The scene of the crime, where the murders were committed, was at Tuttle Hill, south of the city of Ypsilanti. The murders had been carried out just off Tuttle Hill Road, near the Huron River. At the time, Henry Ford was in the process of buying the land surrounding the site. In 1931, Ford had a dam built across the Huron River to provide hydroelectric power to one of his factories, creating what is now Ford Lake. The murder scene is now at the bottom of Ford Lake.

BIBLIOGRAPHY

Ann Arbor News. "Four Found Slain, Burned in Parked Car." August 11, 1931.

———. "Finds Blood on Brothers' Club." August 12, 1931.

———. "Girls Described as Studious and Church Workers." August 12, 1931.

———. "Mysterious Stranger Sought in Slaying." August 12, 1931.

———. "Victim's Purse Found Miles from Bodies." August 12, 1931.

———. "Wounds and Fractured Bonds Found on Bodies Indicate Fierce Battle." August 12, 1931.

———. "Cleveland Seizes Suspect." August 13, 1931.

———. "Confessions, Fifth Extra." August 13, 1931.

———. "Ex-Convict Held as Slayer." August 13, 1931.

———. "Life Sentences Imposed Killers to Marquette, Seventh Extra." August 13, 1931.

———. "Slayer's Gun Is Identified." August 13, 1931.

———. "Three Killers Confess Rushed to Jail Here, Sixth Extra." August 13, 1931.

———. "Two Held in Four Slayings." August 13, 1931.

———. "Voorhies Explains His Transfer of Case; No Criticism Is Implied." August 13, 1931.

———. "Wayne Given Slaying Inquiry." August 13, 1931.

———. "Ypsilanti Chief Tells of Trail to Death Confessions." August 13, 1931.

———. "Appalling Story of Brutality Is Related in Court." August 14, 1931.

———. "Blackstone Shows Regret Over Slayings as Ann Arbor Throng Delays Removal to Jackson." August 14, 1931.

———. "Crowd Perils Killers on Way to Court and After Their Sentence." August 14, 1931.
———. "Fiends in Human Form, Says Judge." August 14, 1931.
———. "Slayers Behind Bars for Rest of Lives." August 14, 1931.
———. "'Smith's Girl' Admits Riding with Killer." August 14, 1931.
———. "Smith's Sweetheart Faces Possible Charge of Being an Accessory." August 14, 1931.
———. "Theft of Liquor Produced First Clew in Slaying." August 14, 1931.
———. "Trip to Jackson Is Made Without Trouble on Road." August 14, 1931.
———. "Girl and Man Jailed When Stained Clothing and Gun Are Found by Authorities." August 15, 1931.
———. "Many Pigs Are Closed During Killing Inquiry." August 15, 1931.
———. "Ypsilanti Chief Objects as Deputies Raid Otis Oden's Residence." August 15, 1931.
———. "Four Men and Woman Still in Jail Here." August 17, 1931.
———. "Behrendt Explains He Didn't Want State to Guide Slaying Inquiry." August 17, 1931.
———. "Six Are Held at Jail Here." August 18, 1931.
———. "Torch Killers Start Trip to Marquette." August 20, 1931.
———. "Smith's Girl Is Arraigned as Accessory." August 22, 1931.
———. "Question Trio in Marquette Prison." August 26, 1931.
———. "Vasher Tells of Activities in Confession." August 29, 1931.
———. "Grand Jury Inquiry Ordered." September 6, 1931.
———. "Witnesses Listed for Grand Jury Inquiry." September 7, 1931.
———. "Keller Trial Is Ordered in Circuit Court." September 24, 1931.
———. "Witnesses Called in Grand Jury Inquiry." September 28, 1931.
———. "Judge's Body Examined for Traces of Poison." September 30, 1931.
———. "Torch Murder Convict Asks for New Trial." July 18, 1949.
———. "Oliver Submits New Trial Data." February 7, 1950.
———. "Oliver to Renew Fight for Retrial." March 3, 1950.
———. "Oliver Denied Retrial in Torch Murder Case." March 4, 1950.
———. "Court Rules Torch-Slayer Was Given Fair Trial." March 10, 1950.
———. "Affidavit Says Witness Saw Bruises on Torch-Murderer." March 23, 1950.
———. "Stephenson Says Oliver Beaten." July 7, 1950.
Ann Arbor Tribune. "4 Youths Found Slain and Cremated in Car." August 12, 1931.
———. "Judge Sample Declares 'Life' Inadequate for Three Killers Given Four Life Terms Apiece." August 14, 1931.

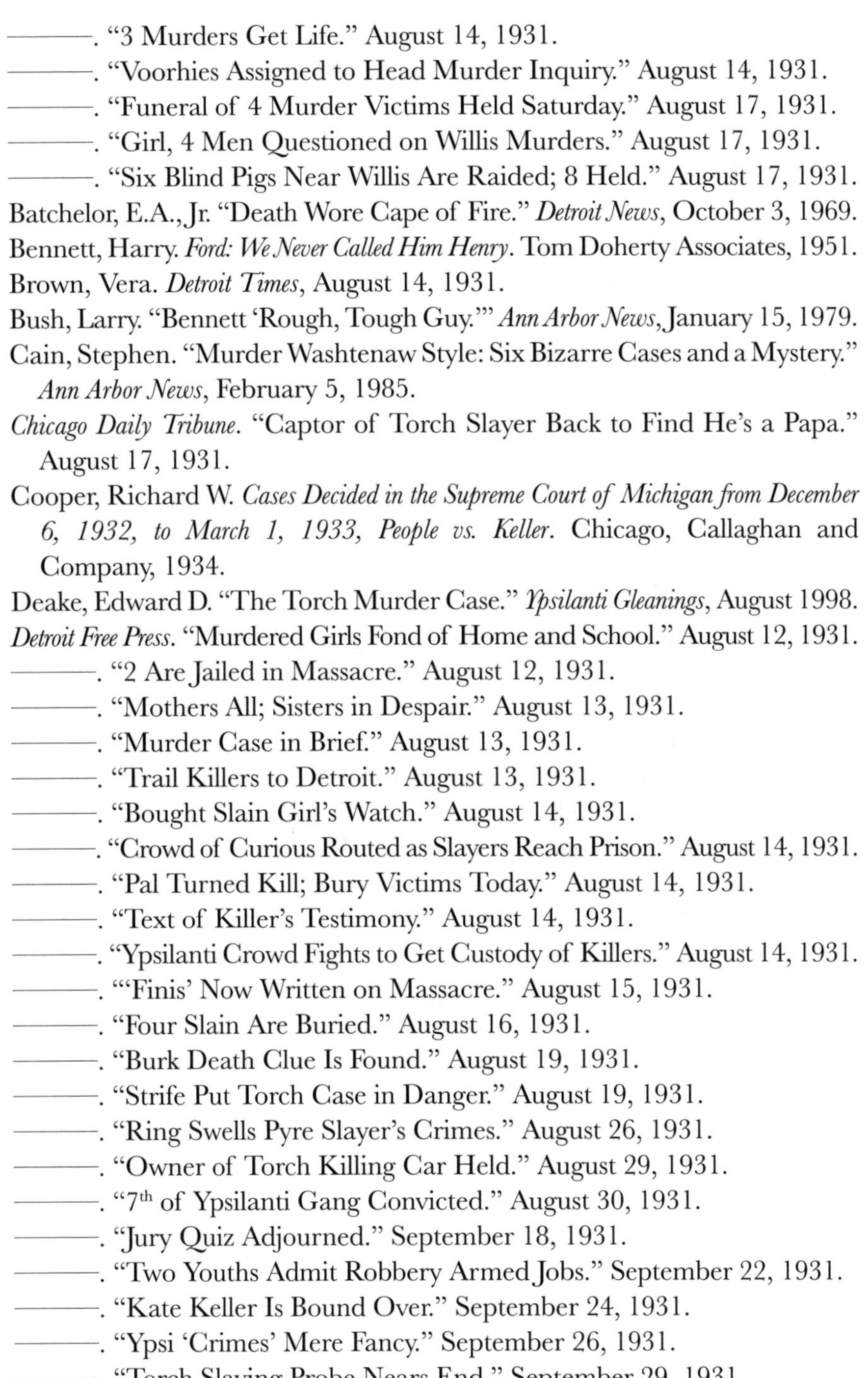

———. "3 Murders Get Life." August 14, 1931.
———. "Voorhies Assigned to Head Murder Inquiry." August 14, 1931.
———. "Funeral of 4 Murder Victims Held Saturday." August 17, 1931.
———. "Girl, 4 Men Questioned on Willis Murders." August 17, 1931.
———. "Six Blind Pigs Near Willis Are Raided; 8 Held." August 17, 1931.
Batchelor, E.A., Jr. "Death Wore Cape of Fire." *Detroit News*, October 3, 1969.
Bennett, Harry. *Ford: We Never Called Him Henry*. Tom Doherty Associates, 1951.
Brown, Vera. *Detroit Times*, August 14, 1931.
Bush, Larry. "Bennett 'Rough, Tough Guy.'" *Ann Arbor News*, January 15, 1979.
Cain, Stephen. "Murder Washtenaw Style: Six Bizarre Cases and a Mystery." *Ann Arbor News*, February 5, 1985.
Chicago Daily Tribune. "Captor of Torch Slayer Back to Find He's a Papa." August 17, 1931.
Cooper, Richard W. *Cases Decided in the Supreme Court of Michigan from December 6, 1932, to March 1, 1933, People vs. Keller*. Chicago, Callaghan and Company, 1934.
Deake, Edward D. "The Torch Murder Case." *Ypsilanti Gleanings*, August 1998.
Detroit Free Press. "Murdered Girls Fond of Home and School." August 12, 1931.
———. "2 Are Jailed in Massacre." August 12, 1931.
———. "Mothers All; Sisters in Despair." August 13, 1931.
———. "Murder Case in Brief." August 13, 1931.
———. "Trail Killers to Detroit." August 13, 1931.
———. "Bought Slain Girl's Watch." August 14, 1931.
———. "Crowd of Curious Routed as Slayers Reach Prison." August 14, 1931.
———. "Pal Turned Kill; Bury Victims Today." August 14, 1931.
———. "Text of Killer's Testimony." August 14, 1931.
———. "Ypsilanti Crowd Fights to Get Custody of Killers." August 14, 1931.
———. "'Finis' Now Written on Massacre." August 15, 1931.
———. "Four Slain Are Buried." August 16, 1931.
———. "Burk Death Clue Is Found." August 19, 1931.
———. "Strife Put Torch Case in Danger." August 19, 1931.
———. "Ring Swells Pyre Slayer's Crimes." August 26, 1931.
———. "Owner of Torch Killing Car Held." August 29, 1931.
———. "7th of Ypsilanti Gang Convicted." August 30, 1931.
———. "Jury Quiz Adjourned." September 18, 1931.
———. "Two Youths Admit Robbery Armed Jobs." September 22, 1931.
———. "Kate Keller Is Bound Over." September 24, 1931.
———. "Ypsi 'Crimes' Mere Fancy." September 26, 1931.
———. "Torch Slaying Probe Nears End." September 29, 1931.

———. "Body Will Be Exhumed." September 30, 1931.
———. "Deputy Chosen for Squires Post." September 30, 1931.
———. "'Mule' Seller's Wife Is Jailed." October 1, 1931.
———. "Will Quiz Torch Killer in Prison." October 2, 1931.
———. "Wife of Torch Rum Seller Serves Time." October 3, 1931.
———. "Torch Murders Witness Writes." October 7, 1931.
———. "Keller Jury Is Complete." October 9, 1931.
———. "Girl Is Linked with Killers." October 10, 1931.
———. "Testify Girl Aided Slayer." October 13, 1931.
———. "Kate Gives Her Story." October 14, 1931.
———. "Keller Case Is Near Jury." October 16, 1931.
———. "Pyre Death Aide Guilty." October 17, 1931.
———. "No Poison Sign Found." October 23, 1931.
———. "Kate Keller Gets 5 Years." October 25, 1931.
———. "Kate Keller Held by Detroit Police." June 13, 1934.
Detroit News. "2 Girls and 1 Boys Found Slain in Auto." August 11, 1931.
———. "Bullet, Blows Are Revealed by Autopsies." August 13, 1931.
———. "4 Victims Were Seen in Milan at 3 A.M." August 13, 1931.
———. "Mother Broken by Tragedy, Tries to Comfort Another." August 13, 1931.
———. "Gun Suspect Held; Second Man Grilled." August 14, 1931.
———. "The Confessions and the Sentence." August 15, 1931.
———. "Girl's Pistol Lately Fired." August 15, 1931.
———. "Judge's Statement." August 15, 1931.
———. "3 Slayers in Cells for 12 Life Terms." August 15, 1931.
———. "Toy Picks Man to Get Reward." August 15, 1931.
Detroit Times. "4 Slain, Cremated in Car." August 11, 1931.
———. "Fiend Killers Reveal Details of Crime." August 14, 1931.
———. "Killers Break as Mob Howls Outside Jail." August 14, 1931.
———. "Only a Dream, but It Led to the Capture of Three Torch Killers." August 14, 1931.
———. "Police Link Heiress in 4 Torch Killings." August 14, 1931.
———. "Torch Killers Crime Career Began Early." August 14, 1931.
———. "'Michigan Worst Crime' Details by the Clock." August 16, 1931.
———. "2 Pals of Torch Killers Seized in Seven Petting Party Holdups; Gov. Brucker Opens War on Pigs." August 16, 1931.
———. "25 Pigs Raided in State Rum Campaign." August 18, 1931.
———. "Charged with Harboring Slayer After Crime." August 22, 1931.
———. "Grill Torch Killers on Other Crimes." August 24, 1931.

———. "Police Confer with Deputy in Probe." August 26, 1931.
———. "Admits Guilt in Torch Quiz." August 29, 1931.
———. "Torch Killers Pals Jailed." September 1, 1931.
———. "One Man Grand Jury to Probe Part in Death of 4." September 5, 1931.
———. "Seek to Indict Torch Girl." September 5, 1931.
———. "23 Called in Keller Quiz." September 8, 1931.
———. "Jury to Decide Torch Girl Case." September 12, 1931.
———. "Keller Torch Probe Set." September 16, 1931.
———. "Torch Killing Car in Show." September 18, 1931.
———. "Torch Slayer Accused in 2d Killing." September 22, 1931.
———. "Deputy Fired in Torch Case." September 26, 1931.
———. "Keller Jury Probe Opens." September 28, 1931.
———. "Quiz Torch Girl in Death." September 29, 1931.
———. "Torch Killer's Girl on Trial Next Week." October 2, 1931.
———. "Waits Probers in Torch Quiz." October 5, 1931.
———. "Keller Trial Opens; Demand Venue Change." October 8, 1931.
———. "Seek to Show Heiress Was 'Jekyll-Hyde.'" October 10, 1931.
———. "Blind Mother to Testify at Torch Trial." October 12, 1931.
———. "But Is Called 'Root of Evil' for Crimes." October 14, 1931.
———. "Torch Killer's Girl Tells of Her Love." October 15, 1931.
———. "Torch Girl Jokes as Prison Looms." October 17, 1931.
———. "Keller's Term Waits Report." October 19, 1931.
———. "Kate Keller Gets 4 Years, Fights Term." October 25, 1931.
———. "Kate to Fight for New Trial." October 26, 1931.
———. "Kate Keller Released." May 3, 1933.
———. "Kate Keller: 2 Pals Held in Holdups." June 13, 1934.
———. "Estate Tangle Harks Back to Torch Murder." December 1, 1935.
Epstein, Clifford. "How a 'Vision' in the Night Led to Solution of Killings." *Detroit News*, August 15, 1931.
Esmond, J.J. "'Kill Them' Cry Heard." *Detroit Free Press*, August 14, 1931.
Fourier, Gregory. *Terror in Ypsilanti: John Norman Collins Unmasked.* Wheatmark, 2016.
George, Hub M. "Sentences 'Too Light.'" *Detroit Free Press*, August 14, 1931.
Girardin, Ray. *Detroit Times*. August 13, 1931.
———. "Accuse Killer's Girl of 4 Torch Murders." *Detroit Times*, August 22, 1931.
———. "Slayer's Girl Stands Mute in Torch Case." *Detroit Times*, August 23, 1931.

Gomberg, E.R. "Guard Killers Against Suicide." *Detroit Times*, August 14, 1931.

Harrison, Eileen. "Makes Use of Prison Time." *Ypsilanti Press*, March 19, 1967

Hilligan, Earl J. "Fred Smith, Frank Oliver and David Blackstone Must Serve Four Consecutive Terms for States Most Atrocious Offense." *Ann Arbor Daily News*, August 14, 1931.

LaRouche, F.W. "Henry Ford's Man Bennett." *Ann Arbor News*, 1930.

Michigan Daily. "The Michigan Daily Mother of Torch Killer to Appear in Secret Hearing." September 29, 1931.

———. "Catherine Keller Testifies to Jury Probing Her Guilt." October 2, 1931.

———. "Katherine Keller Faces Trial for Harboring Killer." October 7, 1931.

———. "Keller to Face Court Quiz Here." October 8, 1931.

———. "Woman Chosen for Jury Duty in Keller Trial." October 9, 1931.

———. "Trial of Katherine Keller Opens as Testimony Begins." October 10, 1931.

———. "Kate Keller, in Court, Faces State's Attempt to Break Down Her Character." October 13, 1931.

———. "Katherine Keller Takes Stand: Makes Testimony in Own Defense." October 14, 1931.

———. "Kate Keller Fails to Get New Trial." December 5, 1931.

Mulcaby, John. "From Street Brawler to Ruthless Enforcer of Ford's Rules." *Ann Arbor News*, September 14, 1997.

Reynolds, Cynthia Furlong. "Lynch Law on Huron Street." *Ann Arbor Observer*, January 2017.

Russell, Floyd R. "Trailing the Torch Killers." *Actual Detective*, October 1938.

Schouman, Fred. "Kate Keller's Case to Jury." *Detroit Times*, October 16, 1931.

———. "Kate Keller Waits Term." *Detroit Times*, October 17, 1931.

Shackman, Grace. "The Three Courthouses of Washtenaw County." *Ann Arbor Observer*, October 1990.

State of Michigan, In the Circuit Court for the County of Washtenaw, The People of the State of Michigan vs. Fred Smith, David Blackstone, and Frank Oliver.

Treml, William B. "Recent Deaths Stir Memories of 'Torch Murders.'" *Ann Arbor News*, April 26, 1967.

———. "County Thrown in Uproar Over 'Torch' Murders 26 Years Ago." *Ann Arbor News*, August 7, 1957.

———. "How Bennett Meddled in Murders." *Ann Arbor News*, January 21, 1979.

Trohan, Walter. "Seize 2 for Motor Slaying." *Chicago Daily Tribune*, August 12, 1931.

———. "Girl's Missing Watch Clew in Motor Slayings." *Chicago Daily Tribune*, August 13, 1931.

———. "Life for 3 Torch Slayers." *Chicago Daily Tribune*, August 14, 1931.

———. "2 More Held as Possible Aids in Torch Slayings." *Chicago Daily Tribune*, August 18, 1931.

Wineberg, Susan Cee. *Lost Ann Arbor*. Arcadia Publishing, 2004.

Ypsilanti Daily Press. "Darwin Curtiss Former Justice Called by Death." February 2, 1931.

———. "Four Drown, One Killed in Crash Near Here." July 30, 1931.

———. "Brucker Orders Voorhies to Direct Crime Investigation." August 12, 1931.

———. "Relief for Broken Lore Family Asked." August 12, 1931.

———. "H. Forwalder Sought." August 13, 1931.

———. "Lore Fund Started Burial Costs Asked." August 13, 1931.

———. "Vivian and Anna, —Just A Couple of Little Kids." August 13, 1931.

———. "De Molays Will Have Charge of Victims Rites." August 14, 1931.

———. "Four Life Terms for Each of Murderers." August 14, 1931.

———. "Fred Smith Killed Pal of Boyhood Fishing Days." August 14, 1931.

———. "'He Was a Rat, I Wish I'd Knifed Him,' Says Nelms." August 14, 1931.

———. "Judge Comments on Smith Record." August 14, 1931.

———. "Kate Keller in Custody as Slayers' Accomplice." August 14, 1931.

———. "Neighbors Sympathetic for Miles Oliver Family." August 14, 1931.

———. "Slayers Guarded." August 14, 1931.

———. "Ypsilanti Center of Most Gruesome Crime on Record." August 14, 1931.

———. "Crime Suspects Rounded Up, Questioned." August 15, 1931.

———. "Girls Burned Alive, Autopsy Today Shows." August 17, 1931.

———. "Check on Outlaw Elements Asked Plans Outlined." August 18, 1931.

———. "Five Raids, One Man Arrested." August 18, 1931.

———. "Gun Sought in River, Forwalder Confesses." August 18, 1931.

———. "Work Secured for Murder Suffered." August 18, 1931.

———. "Detroit Crime May Be Traced to Murder Trio." August 19, 1931.

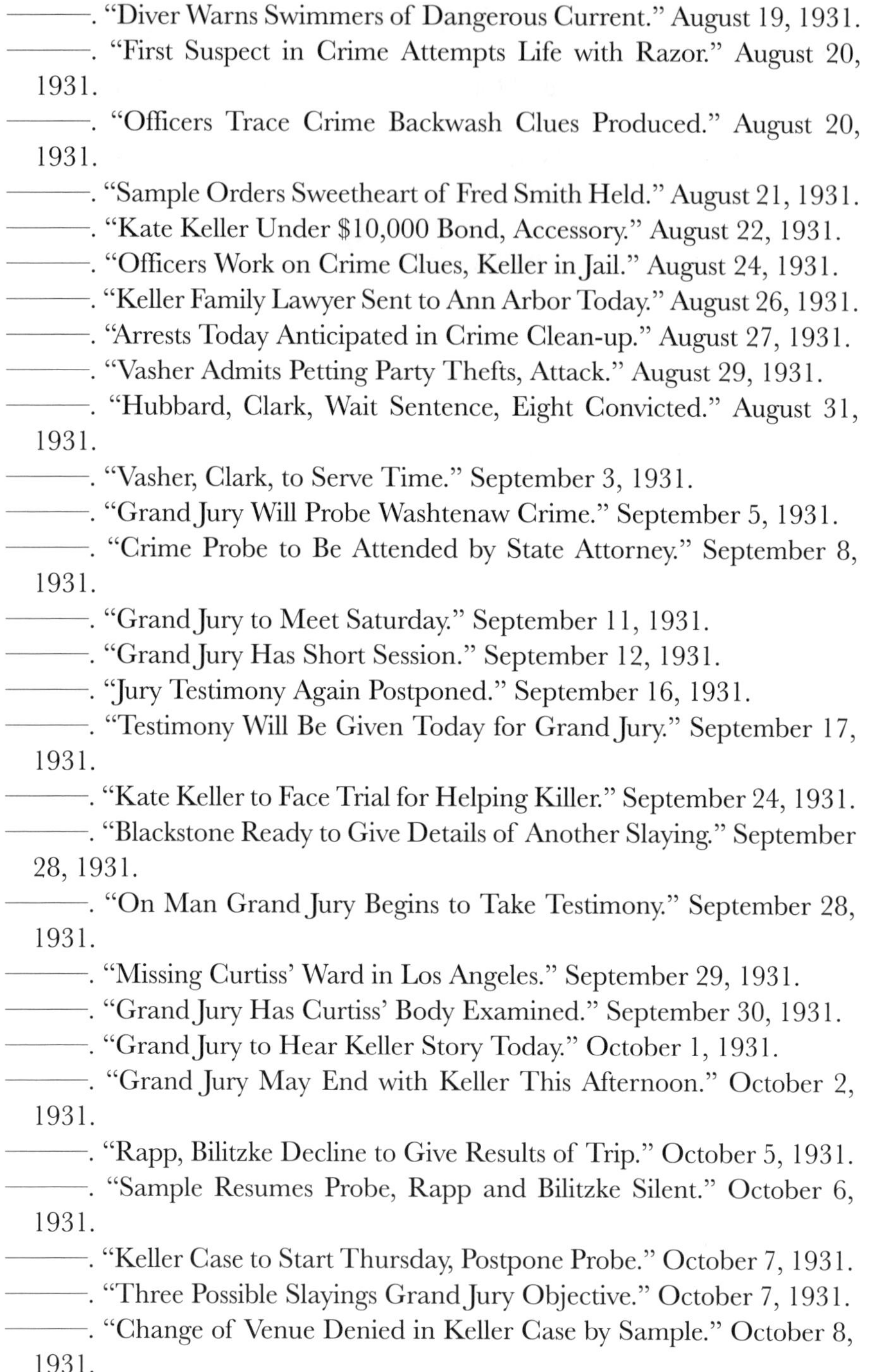

———. "Diver Warns Swimmers of Dangerous Current." August 19, 1931.
———. "First Suspect in Crime Attempts Life with Razor." August 20, 1931.
———. "Officers Trace Crime Backwash Clues Produced." August 20, 1931.
———. "Sample Orders Sweetheart of Fred Smith Held." August 21, 1931.
———. "Kate Keller Under $10,000 Bond, Accessory." August 22, 1931.
———. "Officers Work on Crime Clues, Keller in Jail." August 24, 1931.
———. "Keller Family Lawyer Sent to Ann Arbor Today." August 26, 1931.
———. "Arrests Today Anticipated in Crime Clean-up." August 27, 1931.
———. "Vasher Admits Petting Party Thefts, Attack." August 29, 1931.
———. "Hubbard, Clark, Wait Sentence, Eight Convicted." August 31, 1931.
———. "Vasher, Clark, to Serve Time." September 3, 1931.
———. "Grand Jury Will Probe Washtenaw Crime." September 5, 1931.
———. "Crime Probe to Be Attended by State Attorney." September 8, 1931.
———. "Grand Jury to Meet Saturday." September 11, 1931.
———. "Grand Jury Has Short Session." September 12, 1931.
———. "Jury Testimony Again Postponed." September 16, 1931.
———. "Testimony Will Be Given Today for Grand Jury." September 17, 1931.
———. "Kate Keller to Face Trial for Helping Killer." September 24, 1931.
———. "Blackstone Ready to Give Details of Another Slaying." September 28, 1931.
———. "On Man Grand Jury Begins to Take Testimony." September 28, 1931.
———. "Missing Curtiss' Ward in Los Angeles." September 29, 1931.
———. "Grand Jury Has Curtiss' Body Examined." September 30, 1931.
———. "Grand Jury to Hear Keller Story Today." October 1, 1931.
———. "Grand Jury May End with Keller This Afternoon." October 2, 1931.
———. "Rapp, Bilitzke Decline to Give Results of Trip." October 5, 1931.
———. "Sample Resumes Probe, Rapp and Bilitzke Silent." October 6, 1931.
———. "Keller Case to Start Thursday, Postpone Probe." October 7, 1931.
———. "Three Possible Slayings Grand Jury Objective." October 7, 1931.
———. "Change of Venue Denied in Keller Case by Sample." October 8, 1931.

———. "First Witness Called Today in Keller Hearing." October 9, 1931.
———. "Keller Trial to Reopen Monday, Several Testify." October 10, 1931.
———. "Statements of Keller Woman Repeated Today." October 12, 1931.
———. "Missing Jewels Introduced into Keller Hearing." October 14, 1931.
———. "Keller Trial in Last Stages as Kate Testifies." October 15, 1931.
———. "Kate Keller Found Guilty as Accessory." October 16, 1931.
———. "Delay on Keller Sentence." October 17, 1931.
———. "Mother of Smith Bitter as Story Is Told in Court." October 17, 1931.
———. "Will of Curtiss May Be Tested by Legal Heirs." October 19, 1931.
———. "D.Z. Curtiss Not Poisoned Autopsy Shows." October 22, 1931.
———. "Keller Given Term." October 24, 1931.
———. "Kate Keller to Be Good During Term in Prison." October 26, 1931.
———. "Kate Keller to Seek New Trial." November 2, 1931.
———. "Keller Attorney Asks New Trial, Alleges Errors." November 4, 1931.
———. "Keller Appeal Not to Be Heard Monday." November 5, 1931.
———. "Keller Retrial Plea Heard This Morning." November 14, 1931.
———. "Katherine Keller Allowed Delay in Presenting Appeal." January 7, 1932.
———. "Kate Keller Conviction Set Aside." January 3, 1933.
Ypsilanti Press. "Parole Urged for Surviving 'Torch Murderer.'" October 13, 1967.
———. "Parole Bid for Oliver Submitted." November 29, 1967.
———. "Torch Slayer Parole Still in Question." February 15, 1968.

ABOUT THE AUTHOR

James Thomas Mann is a local historian in Ypsilanti, Michigan, and is the author of ten published books on local history. His works include *Wicked Washtenaw County*, *Wicked Ann Arbor* and *Wicked Ypsilanti*. His most recent work is *Murder and Mayhem in Washtenaw County*. He is also a frequent contributor to the *Ypsilanti Gleanings*, a publication of the Ypsilanti Historical Society. Mann is the host of the Highland Cemetery Lantern Tours every October.